BOOKS BY *John Clancy*

John Clancy's Favorite Recipes (1986)
John Clancy's Christmas Cookbook (1982)
John Clancy's Fish Cookery (1979)
John Clancy's Oven Cookery
(with Frances Field) (1976)
John Clancy's Baking Book (1975)

JOHN CLANCY'S
FAVORITE
RECIPES

JOHN CLANCY'S
FAVORITE
RECIPES

JOHN CLANCY

ILLUSTRATIONS BY
IRRA VERBITSKY

ATHENEUM *New York* **1986**

Library of Congress Cataloging-in-Publication Data

Clancy, John.
John Clancy's favorite recipes.

Includes index.
1. Cookery.   I. Title.   II. Title: Favorite recipes.
TX715.C57635   1986   641.5   85-48148
ISBN 0-689-11710-8

Published simultaneously in Canada by Collier Macmillan Canada, Inc.
Composition by Maryland Linotype Composition Co., Inc., Baltimore, Maryland
Manufactured by Fairfield Graphics, Fairfield, Pennsylvania
Designed by Cathryn S. Aison
FIRST EDITION

FOR
Wendy Afton Rieder,

WHO WILL ALWAYS BE A LEADING LADY.
WITH MUCH GRATITUDE AND AFFECTION

CONTENTS

$\mathscr{I}$NTRODUCTION

The repertoire of recipes offered here is based on my own many years in the kitchen.

Most of those recipes bring fond memories of the places I have been and the people I have met through the years. I am happy to say I am still in touch with many of them.

After training with Rudolf Standish (a well-known caterer) and James Beard for two years, I was invited to take charge of the kitchen at Chillingsworth, a small restaurant on Cape Cod. This was no ordinary restaurant; it was in a charming house built by Captain Chillingsworth in 1723. The tables were set with Royal Crown Derby service plates, sterling flatware, and crystal. It was a commercial extension of the owner's life style.

I arrived at Chillingsworth in October of 1956, giving myself the winter to prepare professionally for the busy late spring and hectic summer season. The restaurant seated thirty-five patrons. Five years and several renovations later we were serving about one hundred seventy-five dinners. This was the result of the very hard work of everyone on hand, not to mention favorable publicity from *Life* magazine, the *New York Times*, and the *Boston Globe*. Besides the hard work, it was great fun and a wonderful learning experience.

This led me into the research and development division of the Green Giant Company. I would spend two weeks each month in the plant, which is located in Le Sueur, Minnesota. After several months—and many days at forty below zero—I left to accept a position as chef at the Coach House restaurant in Greenwich Village, in March 1962.

When Mr. Lainides, the proprietor, bought the restaurant, the establishment was operated like a tearoom. He wanted to upgrade the menu, and we worked together for two years to achieve that end.

I next worked as chef consultant for a caterer and several small New York restaurants.

In February of 1967 I joined the books division of Time/Life as test kitchen chef for the Foods of the World series—an experience that broadened my repertoire, allowed me to pass on newly discovered recipes to the students at John Clancy's Kitchen Workshop (opened in March of 1978), and certainly influenced the eclectic menu I planned for my own restaurant.

When John Clancy's restaurant opened on April 14, 1981, it became the first on the East Coast to grill over mesquite.

After all these years, there have been many changes in the American kitchen. The professionalism of preparation and the inventiveness of the new generation of cooks and chefs are more exciting than ever before. The availability and quality of fresh and packaged ingredients are staggering. Every time I see shallots in the local supermarket, I think back to the days when they were available only by mail order.

Taking advantage of this abundance, the recipe introductions throughout this book suggest possible variations on preparation, seasoning, and serving. If you think of a recipe as a guide to preparing a dish and not as a formula that you must follow (except for timing, weights, and measurements), it will open new doors for your own creativity, allowing you self-expression in the kitchen, and an opportunity to display your own style and flair.

I hope you enjoy this collection of recipes as much as I enjoyed cooking them.

John Clancy
FEBRUARY 1986

HORS D'OEUVRES AND APPETIZERS

CHICKEN HEARTS TERIYAKI

Because the cooking time is so short, these chicken hearts are a good idea for a large cocktail party, indoors or out.

SERVES 4 TO 6

2 teaspoons dry mustard dissolved in 1 teaspoon hot water
1 teaspoon cornstarch dissolved in 2 tablespoons dry sherry
¼ cup Japanese soy sauce
½ cup fresh Chicken Stock (page 48) or canned broth
1 tablespoon sugar
1½ pounds chicken hearts

Combine the dissolved mustard, cornstarch-sherry mixture, soy sauce, chicken broth, and sugar in a small saucepan. Bring the mixture to a simmer, stirring constantly with a wooden spoon until it thickens and becomes clear. Remove from the heat and set aside.

PREHEAT THE BROILER

String the chicken hearts on skewers and broil them 4 inches from the heat for 7 to 8 minutes, turning and brushing them with the sauce intermittently until they are brown and crisp.

SKEWERED BEEF HEART

A beef heart can weigh 4 or 5 pounds, and if you serve it with before-dinner drinks it will serve 10 to 12 people.

If you wish, you may start the day before by marinating the beef heart and storing it in the refrigerator.

SERVES 8

1 *large beef heart (4 to 5 pounds)*
1 *cup red wine vinegar*
1 *tablespoon Tabasco sauce*
1 *tablespoon prepared mustard*
1 *tablespoon finely chopped garlic*
1 *tablespoon ground cumin*
2 *teaspoons salt*

Trim the beef heart of any fat and cut into 1-inch cubes. Combine the vinegar, Tabasco sauce, mustard, garlic, ground cumin, and salt in a small bowl. Mix the ingredients well with a dinner fork. Drop the beef heart cubes into a medium-sized bowl and pour in the marinade.

Marinate the beef heart cubes for 4 hours at room temperature, tossing them every so often.

Light a 2-to-3-inch-thick layer of mesquite or charcoal in a grill. When the coals begin to burn white the heat will be proper for cooking. Or, if you don't have a grill, preheat your oven broiler. String the beef heart cubes on metal skewers and broil 4 inches from the heat for about 4 to 5 minutes, turning the skewers two or three times. Serve the grilled beef heart with the Salsa Cruda sauce on page 288.

$\mathscr{S}$PICED $\mathscr{B}$EEF

This beef will keep in the refrigerator for several weeks. Use it as you would prosciutto or Westphalian ham. Thinly sliced, the spiced beef can be served with cocktails or as a snack anytime.

SERVES 8 TO 10

1/2 *cup dark brown sugar*
2 *tablespoons juniper berries, crushed*
1/2 *cup kosher salt*
1 *tablespoon ground allspice*
1 *tablespoon freshly ground black pepper*
2 *teaspoons ground ginger*
1 *teaspoon ground nutmeg*
1/2 *teaspoon cayenne pepper*
One 4-pound lean fresh brisket

Combine all ingredients except the brisket and mix well. Place the brisket in a large bowl and add the sugar-spice mixture. Turn the meat around in the bowl so it is coated evenly with the mixture. Cover the bowl with plastic wrap and marinate in the refrigerator for 12 days. Turn the meat once each day.

PREHEAT THE OVEN TO 275°F

Remove the meat from the bowl and place in a large, heavy casserole with a tight-fitting cover. Add the liquid that has accumulated in the bowl. Cover the casserole and braise the meat on the lower middle shelf of the oven for 3½ hours, or until the meat is tender.

Remove the meat to a plate and cool to room temperature.

Wrap in foil and refrigerate overnight.

Cut the beef into paper-thin slices.

*M*OUSSE OF *H*AM

If it is possible for you to get tomato paste in a tube, soak the gelatin in 3 tablespoons of ice water, then add 1 tablespoon of the paste to the ingredients in the processor. This saves opening a can of tomato juice.

SERVES 6 TO 8

4 teaspoons unflavored gelatin
¼ cup tomato juice
1½ cups fresh Chicken Stock (page 48) or canned broth
3 cups cubed ham
¼ cup finely chopped celery
2 tablespoons grated onion
1 teaspoon Worcestershire sauce
½ cup whipped heavy cream
Salt and freshly ground black pepper to taste

Soak the gelatin in the tomato juice. In a small, heavy saucepan bring the chicken stock to a boil and stir in the gelatin mixture. Pour the stock into a small bowl and chill in the refrigerator.

Place the cubed ham, celery, grated onion, and Worcestershire sauce in the container of a food processor. Process the ingredients into a smooth mixture. Scrape the mixture into a large bowl. When the chicken jelly is almost set—in 1½ to 2 hours—stir it into the ham mixture, then fold in the whipped cream and season to taste with salt and pepper. Moisten a 1-quart mold with cold water and spoon the ham mousse into the mold. Cover with plastic wrap and chill in the refrigerator for 2 hours before serving.

Hot Anchovy Canapés

If you like a less salty anchovy flavor, wash the anchovies under cold running water, pat dry with paper towels, and proceed with the recipe.

SERVES 8 TO 10

4 ounces flat anchovies
2 teaspoons tomato paste
1 tablespoon olive oil
1 teaspoon finely chopped garlic
2 teaspoons lemon juice
3 teaspoons chopped Italian parsley
1 loaf of French or Italian bread
Freshly ground black pepper to taste

PREHEAT THE OVEN TO 500°F

Drain the anchovies of their oil and place them on a chopping board.

Using a metal spatula, mash the anchovies into a smooth paste. Scrape the anchovy paste into a small bowl. Beat in the tomato paste, olive oil, garlic, lemon juice, and 2 tablespoons of the chopped parsley. Set the mixture aside.

Slice 10 pieces of bread ½ inch thick and place them on a cookie sheet.

Under a hot broiler toast the bread on one side only. When the bread is cool enough to handle, spread the untoasted side with the anchovy mixture. Season with freshly ground pepper and bake on the middle shelf of the oven for 10 minutes. Remove the canapés to a serving platter and sprinkle with the remaining 1 teaspoon of chopped parsley.

7

Shrimp Toast

Using very fresh shrimp, the shrimp mixture can be made the day before, covered with plastic wrap, and stored in the refrigerator.

MAKES ABOUT 36 PIECES

1 pound raw shrimp, peeled and deveined
6 canned water chestnuts
¼ cup fresh pork fat, ground
2 tablespoons freshly chopped Chinese parsley or cilantro
2 tablespoons dry sherry
1½ teaspoons salt
2 medium-sized eggs
¼ cup cornstarch
9 slices white bread
3 cups peanut or vegetable oil

With a large, sharp knife, chop the shrimp and water chestnuts together until they turn into a fine pulp. Place in a medium-sized bowl. Add the ground pork fat, Chinese parsley, dry sherry, salt, eggs, and cornstarch. Beat the ingredients together with a large spoon until they are well blended. With a bread knife, remove the crusts from the white bread and cut the slices diagonally into triangles.

With a small metal spatula, divide the shrimp mixture evenly among the bread triangles, mounding it slightly in the center.

PREHEAT THE OVEN TO WARM

Fill a large cast-iron skillet two-thirds full of peanut or vegetable oil. Using a deep-fat-frying thermometer heat the oil to 375°F. Gently drop the triangles 6 to 8 at a time shrimp side down into the hot oil and with a slotted spoon turn them over and continue to fry until the bread is golden brown. Remove the triangles from the oil and transfer them to a baking pan lined with paper towels. Keep them warm until the remaining shrimp toast has been fried.

$\mathscr{C}$EVICHE

Besides being a refreshing first course, Ceviche is good for large gatherings when served in small scallop shells.

Serve the Ceviche on a bed of lettuce garnished with sliced tomato and sprigs of cilantro. Using fresh bay scallops in place of the fish is equally good. The Ceviche can also be garnished with very thin slices of fresh hot chilies.

SERVES 4 TO 6

¾ cup fresh lemon juice
¾ cup fresh lime juice
¼ teaspoon dried red pepper flakes, crushed
2 red onions, sliced paper thin
¼ teaspoon chopped garlic
1 teaspoon freshly chopped cilantro
1 teaspoon salt
Freshly ground black pepper to taste
1½ pounds fillet of gray sole

In a large glass or stainless steel bowl, mix the lemon juice, lime juice, crushed red pepper flakes, sliced red onion, chopped garlic, cilantro, salt, and freshly ground black pepper.

Place the fish on a cutting board and with a sharp knife cut the fish crosswise into ½-inch strips. Place the strips in the marinade and gently toss the fish so it is evenly mixed with the sliced onion. Cover the bowl with plastic wrap and refrigerate for about 2½ to 3 hours, or until the fish turns white.

$\mathscr{S}$HRIMP $\mathscr{B}$ALLS

Shrimp Balls are a good choice for a large party. They can be made weeks in advance, wrapped, and stored in the freezer.

MAKES APPROXIMATELY 36 BALLS

1 pound potatoes, peeled
6 tablespoons butter
1½ cups grated mild cheddar cheese
1 egg yolk
¼ cup chopped parsley
1 cup fresh chopped scallions
2 teaspoons salt
¼ teaspoon cayenne pepper
1½ pounds cooked shrimp, coarsely chopped
2 eggs, lightly beaten
2 cups Fresh Bread Crumbs, or more as needed (recipe follows)
Vegetable oil for deep-fat frying

Cook the potatoes in boiling salted water for about 20 minutes, or until tender. Drain the potatoes in a colander. Return the potatoes to the pot and shake the pot back and forth over high heat until they are rid of all their moisture.

Place the cooked potatoes, butter, cheese, egg yolk, parsley, scallions, salt, and cayenne pepper into the container of a food processor and process until the potatoes are smooth and all the ingredients are well blended.

Using a rubber spatula, scape the contents of the container into a large bowl. Mix in the cooked shrimp, cover the bowl, and refrigerate the mixture for about 1 hour before shaping.

To shape each ball, flour your hands lightly and using about 2 heaping tablespoons for each one, shape the mixture into balls, placing each one on a jelly roll pan as it is formed.

One by one, dip the shrimp balls into the beaten eggs, then roll each one in the bread crumbs. Return to the refrigerator to chill. Fill a deep-fat fryer or a cast-iron skillet with vegetable oil to a depth of about 3½ to 4 inches and heat to 375° F.

Fry the shrimp balls 6 to 8 at a time for about 3 to 4 minutes, or until golden brown.

Drain on paper towels.

FRESH BREAD CRUMBS

The bread you use can be up to four days old. Each slice of white bread (not thin-sliced) with crust removed will yield about ½ cup of crumbs.

MAKES ABOUT 2 CUPS

4 slices white bread, crusts removed

Cut the bread into small pieces and place in the container of a food processor. Process the bread by turning the machine on and off until the bread turns into crumbs.

CHERRYSTONE CLAMS
WITH ASPIC

This is a recipe out of my past. We served them at Chillingsworth on Cape Cod, where they were called Clams en Gelée. Every so often I put them on the menu in my restaurant. It's best to buy the clams the day before they are needed. Scrub them clean under cold running water and store them undisturbed in the refrigerator overnight. The clams will relax and be easier to open.

SERVES 4

2 tablespoons unflavored gelatin
½ cup cold water
2½ cups fresh Chicken Stock (page 48) or canned broth
2 large garlic cloves, crushed with the flat side of a cleaver
¼ cup finely chopped celery
2 egg whites beaten to a froth
2 egg shells, crushed
2 tablespoons chopped parsley
24 cherrystone clams on the half shell

Mix the gelatin in the cold water to soften. Combine the chicken stock, garlic, chopped celery, egg whites, egg shells, and softened gelatin in a 1-quart saucepan. Set the pan over high heat and bring the liquid to a boil, stirring constantly. Reduce the heat to low and simmer the stock for 10 minutes undisturbed. Strain the stock into a bowl through a cheesecloth-lined sieve. Allow the stock to drain undisturbed.

Set the bowl of stock in a larger bowl of crushed ice and stir very gently with a metal spoon until the stock becames a thick syrup. Stir in the chopped parsley, pour the mixture into a shallow platter, and place it in the refrigerator to set.

Before serving the clams, invert the layer of aspic onto a clean surface. Put a hot towel on the platter and the aspic will drop out. Remove the platter and with a large knife chop the aspic into a very small dice. Heap the aspic on top of the clams and serve at once.

Tricolor Mousse

Not too long ago, recipes like this one would have taken hours to assemble. Thanks to the invention of the food processor, it's almost like magic.

This very pretty mousse makes a wonderful first course or a main course for luncheon. It can be served hot with a Hollandaise Sauce (page 293) or cold with an herbed mayonnaise.

SERVES 10 TO 12

SALMON MOUSSE

12 ounces fillet of salmon
1 tablespoon egg white
1½ teaspoons salt
⅛ teaspoon cayenne pepper
½ cup heavy cream
½ cup heavy cream, whipped

SOLE MOUSSE

1 bunch watercress
4 large scallions
2 pounds fillet of sole
1 egg white
1½ cups heavy cream
¼ teaspoon white pepper
1½ teaspoons salt
2 tablespoons butter, softened

TO MAKE THE SALMON MOUSSE

Cut the salmon fillets into 1-inch pieces and purée in a food processor. Add the egg white, salt, cayenne, and ½ cup of heavy cream, and purée until

14

smooth. Scrape the mixture into a small bowl. Fold the whipped cream into the salmon mixture. Place the mousse in the freezer to firm before spreading in the mold.

TO MAKE THE SOLE MOUSSE

Wash the watercress and pick the leaves from the stems. Bring a small saucepan of water to a boil and drop in the leaves to blanch. Immediately remove the saucepan from the heat, cover the top with a large sieve, and place under cold running water. Drain the water from the pan and dry the leaves with paper towels. Coarsely chop the green tops of four large scallions.

Cut the sole fillets into 1-inch pieces and purée in a food processor. When the puréed sole is free of any small lumps, add the egg white, heavy cream, pepper, and salt. Purée only until they are all combined. Scrape half of this purée into a small bowl and place in the freezer until firm. To the remaining purée add the watercress leaves and scallion tops and purée in the food processor. Place this mixture in the freezer to firm.

TO ASSEMBLE THE TRICOLOR MOUSSE
PREHEAT THE OVEN TO 350°F

When the three mousses are firm enough to spread easily, remove them from the freezer. With the softened butter, coat the inside of a 3 x 3½ x 4-inch pâté mold with removable sides and bottom. Cover and seal the outside of the mold with aluminum foil. Spread the green mousse of sole across the bottom of the mold, taking care to make the top level and smooth. Spread the plain sole mousse on top of the green, and smooth and level the top. Spread the salmon mousse on top of the plain sole mousse, and again smooth and level the top. Cover and seal the top of the mold with aluminum foil. Place the mold in a roasting pan half filled with hot water in the 350° oven. Bake for about 1¼ hours, or until a knife inserted into the mousse comes out clean. Unmold the mousse onto a large serving platter. With paper towels sponge off any excess liquid that has drained from the mousse.

15

CRABMEAT RÉMOULADE

This rémoulade not only makes a tasty and pretty first course. For a main course, double the recipe and serve two shells per person. The crabmeat can be packed in the shells and covered with the rémoulade sauce hours before serving.

SERVES 4

CRABMEAT

1 pound fresh crabmeat
2 tablespoons dry sherry

RÉMOULADE SAUCE

2 cups fresh Mayonnaise (page 294)
1 teaspoon finely chopped garlic
2 tablespoons finely chopped chives
1 teaspoon dried tarragon
2 tablespoons finely chopped parsley
2 teaspoons prepared mustard
1/4 cup finely chopped gherkins

FINISHING AND GARNISHES

1/3 cup fresh Mayonnaise (page 294)
4 thin slices of tomato
1 hard-cooked egg, chopped
1 tablespoon finely chopped red pepper
1 tablespoon finely chopped green pepper
1 tablespoon finely chopped celery

16

TO PREPARE THE CRABMEAT

Flake the crabmeat into a small bowl and remove any cartilage. Sprinkle the crabmeat with the dry sherry, cover with plastic wrap, and refrigerate.

TO MAKE THE RÉMOULADE SAUCE

Combine all the ingredients in a medium-sized bowl and mix well. Let the rémoulade sauce rest for 2 hours before using.

TO ASSEMBLE THE RÉMOULADE
PREHEAT THE OVEN TO 375°F

Mix the mayonnaise into the flaked crabmeat and divide the mixture evenly among 4 large scallop shells or 4 individual ramekins. Spread the top of the crabmeat with the rémoulade sauce and garnish each serving with a tomato slice. Place on a jelly roll pan and bake in the preheated oven for 12 to 15 minutes, or until bubbly hot.

Combine the chopped egg, red and green peppers, and celery and sprinkle on top of the crabmeat.

Serve on individual plates.

17

$\mathscr{S}$HRIMP $\mathscr{R}$ÉMOULADE

Rémoulade sauce is usually made with a mayonnaise base. This is a Creole rémoulade, and made with fresh shrimp from Louisiana it becomes very special.

SERVES 4 TO 6

3 tablespoons Creole mustard*
4 teaspoons Hungarian paprika
2 teaspoons salt
1/2 teaspoon cayenne pepper
1/3 cup tarragon vinegar
1 1/4 cups olive oil
1 cup chopped scallions
1/2 cup finely chopped celery
1/2 cup chopped flat-leaf parsley
2 pounds small cooked shrimp

Combine the Creole mustard, paprika, salt, cayenne, and vinegar in a large bowl. Beat the ingredients with a wire whisk until they are well blended. Gradually whisk in the olive oil. Stir in the scallions, celery, and parsley. Taste for seasoning, then add the shrimp, stirring them to coat with the rémoulade sauce. Cover with plastic wrap and refrigerate for at least 2 hours before serving.

* Creole mustard can be purchased at most gourmet or specialty food shops.

Baked Oysters on the Half Shell

If you are not opening your own oysters, don't forget to ask your fish store for the deep side of the shells.

SERVES 4

6 tablespoons butter
1½ cups Fresh Bread Crumbs (page 12)
1 teaspoon finely chopped garlic
2 tablespoons chopped flat-leaf parsley
24 large, shucked oysters with 24 deep shells
¼ cup grated imported Parmesan cheese
4 lemon wedges

PREHEAT THE OVEN TO 450°F

Heat 3 tablespoons of the butter in a 8- or 10-inch heavy skillet. Add half the fresh bread crumbs and stir them into the hot butter until they start to color. Add the garlic and continue to stir until the crumbs are crisp. Remove the crumbs to a small bowl, mix in the parsley, and set aside to cool.

With paper towels, wipe the oyster shells dry and place them on a large jelly roll pan. Divide the toasted bread crumbs among the shells and top each one with an oyster. Mix the remaining bread crumbs with the Parmesan cheese and sprinkle on top of the oysters. Dot the oysters with the remaining butter and bake on the top shelf of the oven for 12 to 14 minutes, or until the crumbs are golden brown. Serve immediately on individual plates garnished with a lemon wedge.

*M*USHROOMS *S*TUFFED WITH *C*RABMEAT

We have been serving these stuffed mushrooms at the restaurant since the first day we opened. They are by far the most popular hot appetizer. They can be assembled early in the day and stored in the refrigerator. Just before baking, sprinkle them with the bread crumbs.

SERVES 6 TO 8

2 tablespoons butter
¼ cup finely chopped scallions
3 tablespoons all-purpose flour
1 cup milk
¼ teaspoon salt
⅛ teaspoon cayenne pepper
½ teaspoon fresh lemon juice
12 ounces fresh lump crabmeat
24 2-inch mushroom caps
Salt and freshly ground black pepper
½ cup Fresh Bread Crumbs (page 12)
2 tablespoons chopped parsley

Melt the butter in a small saucepan, add the chopped scallions, and cook for about 2 minutes. Stir in the flour and cook for 2 minutes. Whisk in the milk and bring to a boil, reduce the heat to simmer, and cook for 3 to 5 minutes, or until the sauce is thick enough to coat a spoon. Season with the salt, cayenne pepper, and lemon juice. Set aside.

PREHEAT THE OVEN TO 375°F

Flake the crabmeat into a medium-sized bowl, removing any cartilage. Stir the sauce into the crabmeat, mixing well.

20

Wipe the mushroom caps clean with dampened paper towels. Place them in a small, shallow pan and sprinkle them lightly with salt and pepper. Fill each mushroom cap with the crabmeat mixture and sprinkle with the bread crumbs. Bake in the preheated oven for about 20 minutes or until you can pierce the caps easily with the point of a paring knife. Sprinkle with the chopped parsley, and serve on a warm platter.

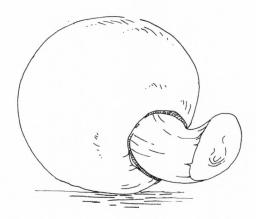

*M*ARINATED *M*USHROOMS

These crisp, wonderful-tasting mushrooms keep safely in the refrigerator for up to 3 weeks. Serve them on a bed of lettuce for a first course or stick them with toothpicks for cocktail parties. Packed in an old Mason jar, they also make a nice gift for the weekend host or hostess.

SERVES 6 TO 8

1½ pounds fresh button mushroom caps
1½ cups dry white wine
1½ cups olive oil
1 teaspoon Tabasco sauce
2 tablespoons Worcestershire sauce
2 teaspoons salt
4 tablespoons finely chopped onion
1 tablespoon finely chopped garlic
1 lemon, thinly sliced
¼ cup chopped parsley

Wipe the mushroom caps clean with damp paper towels and drop them into a glass or ceramic bowl. In a stainless steel mixing bowl, combine the white wine, olive oil, Tabasco sauce, Worcestershire sauce, salt, onion, and garlic. Beat this marinade mixture with a wire whisk until the ingredients are well blended. Pour over the mushroom caps and mix in the sliced lemon. Cover with plastic wrap and store in the refrigerator for at least two days. Just before serving, stir in the chopped parsley.

STUFFED MUSHROOMS ITALIAN STYLE

Joe's Restaurant on MacDougal Street in Greenwich Village, where I have dined well for over 20 years, was the inspiration for this recipe. Since the prosciutto is finely chopped it would be worth asking the butcher if he has any end pieces, which would be less expensive.

SERVES 4 TO 6

½ lemon
12 large mushroom caps
1 cup ricotta cheese
4 thin slices prosciutto, finely chopped
1 egg yolk
1½ teaspoons salt
Freshly ground black pepper to taste
1 tablespoon chopped chives

In a 4-quart pot, bring 3 quarts of water to a boil. Squeeze the lemon into the water and drop in the rind. With paper towels wipe the mushroom caps clean. Place the mushrooms, a few at a time, in a large wire strainer. Lower the strainer into the boiling water and blanch the mushrooms for 30 seconds. Remove and drain the mushrooms on paper towels.

Continue to blanch the remaining mushrooms.

PREHEAT THE OVEN TO 400°F

In a medium-sized bowl, combine the ricotta cheese, prosciutto, egg yolk, salt, pepper, and chopped chives. Mix all the ingredients until well blended. Fill the mushroom caps with the cheese mixture and arrange the caps in a shallow baking dish. Reduce the oven temperature to 375° and bake the stuffed mushroom caps for 6 to 8 minutes, or until the filling begins to bubble.

23

CAPONATA

Caponata has been available in small cans in most supermarkets for as long as I can remember. Making it at home with fresh vegetables, you would never know it was the same dish. Although the recipe calls for chilling the Caponata for 2 to 3 hours, I prefer to make it the day before, removing it from the refrigerator several hours before serving.

MAKES ABOUT 4 CUPS

1 *pound eggplant*
Salt
½ *cup olive oil*
1 *cup finely chopped celery*
1 *cup finely chopped onion*
3 *tablespoons red wine vinegar*
1 *teaspoon sugar*
1½ *cups canned plum tomatoes, drained*
1 *tablespoon tomato paste*
8 *large green olives, pitted and coarsely chopped*
1 *tablespoon capers*
2 *flat anchovies, finely chopped*
Salt and freshly ground black pepper to taste

Peel the eggplant and cut it into ½-inch dice, then place it in a colander and sprinkle with salt. Set the colander on a plate and let the eggplant drain for 30 to 45 minutes. Pat the eggplant dry with paper towels.

Heat ¼ cup of the olive oil in a large skillet (not aluminum or cast iron) and sauté the eggplant until it is lightly browned. Remove the egg-plant to a bowl with a slotted spoon. Add the remaining olive oil to the skillet and cook the celery and onion until soft and lightly colored. Return the eggplant to the skillet and stir in the vinegar, sugar, tomatoes, tomato paste, green olives, capers, anchovies, and salt and freshly ground black pepper to taste. Simmer the mixture for 20 minutes. Remove from the heat and transfer to a serving dish, cover with plastic wrap, and chill in the refrigerator for 2 to 3 hours before serving.

In addition to tasting for salt and pepper before serving, I like to add a splash of vinegar.

GUACAMOLE

There are as many recipes for guacamole as there are avocados hanging from the trees. I sometimes reserve half the avocado and cut it into quarter-inch slices, then quickly stir it into the Guacamole for a little texture.

SERVES 4

2 *large ripe avocados*
2 *tablespoons grated onion*
1 *fresh green chili, chopped*
1 *small tomato, peeled, seeded, and coarsely chopped*
2 *tablespoons fresh cilantro, finely chopped*
½ *teaspoon salt*
Freshly ground black pepper to taste

Cut the avocados in half lengthwise and remove the pits. With a soup spoon, scoop out the flesh of the avocados into a medium-sized bowl, and discard the skins. With a dinner fork, mash the avocado. Add the onion, green chili, tomato, cilantro, salt, and pepper. Cover with plastic wrap (do not use aluminum foil because it will discolor the avocado) and refrigerate for 1 hour before serving.

$\mathscr{V}$EGETABLE $\mathscr{C}$AVIAR

This is a pleasant fresh snack to serve with before-dinner cocktails.
Use any toast or cracker that you would use for cheeses.

MAKES ABOUT 2 CUPS

1 medium-sized eggplant
6 tablespoons olive or vegetable oil
3⁄4 cup chopped onion
1⁄2 cup finely chopped green pepper
1⁄2 teaspoon finely chopped garlic
2 medium-sized tomatoes, blanched, peeled, seeded, and finely chopped
A pinch of sugar
1 1⁄2 teaspoons salt
Freshly ground black pepper to taste
2 tablespoons distilled vinegar

PREHEAT THE OVEN TO 400°F

With a large kitchen fork, prick the eggplant several times. Bake the eggplant in a shallow ovenproof dish for 1 to 1½ hours, or until it is soft.

Heat the oil in a small skillet, add the onion, green peppers, and garlic, and cook the mixture until the vegetables are brown. Add the tomatoes and cook over high heat until the liquid evaporates. Scrape the mixture into a mixing bowl.

When the eggplant is soft, remove from the oven. When it is cool enough to handle, remove the skin and discard it. Mash the eggplant with a fork and stir it into the onion mixture. Add the sugar, salt, pepper, and vinegar and mix well. Cover the bowl with plastic wrap and chill in the refrigerator for 2 hours before serving.

THOUGHTS FOR CROUSTADES

Both these croustades can be frozen before baking. Wrapped well in freezer paper, they will keep safely for 2 to 3 weeks. If you bake them frozen, add about 20 to 30 minutes to the baking time called for in the recipes. When making the lobster croustades (page 31) I sometimes use brandy in place of the sherry and add 2 teaspoons of tomato paste to the filling for a more lobster-like color.

If you happen to have dried mushrooms in your kitchen when making the mushroom croustades (page 28), soak ¼ cup in boiling water until they are soft. Finely chop them and add to the mushroom mixture. This will greatly intensify the flavor of the croustade.

The croustade can be served for brunch along with a simple salad with an oil-vinegar dressing. In this case each croustade will serve 6 people.

As a first course, or with before-dinner drinks, you will easily get 8 to 10 servings.

*C*ROUSTADE OF *M*USHROOMS

SERVES 8 TO 10

FILLING

3 *tablespoons unsalted butter*
2 *tablespoons finely chopped shallots*
1 *pound thinly sliced mushrooms*
4 *tablespoons all-purpose flour*
1 *cup milk mixed with 1 cup heavy cream*
1 *teaspoon salt*
½ *teaspoon freshly ground black pepper*
2 *tablespoons chopped flat-leaf parsley*

PASTRY

¼ pound puff pastry or puff pastry scraps*
1 egg, beaten

TO MAKE THE FILLING

Melt the butter in a heavy skillet, add the shallots, and cook until they are transparent. Add the sliced mushrooms, cover the pan, and cook over medium heat for 10 minutes. Remove the cover and cook the mushrooms over high heat to evaporate the liquid in the skillet.

Lower the heat and, with a wooden spoon, stir in the flour and cook for a few minutes. With a wire whisk, beat in the milk-cream mixture. Add the salt and pepper, bring the mixture to a boil to thicken, reduce the heat to low, and simmer for 5 minutes. Stir in the parsley and scrape the mixture into a shallow dish. Chill the mushroom filling, covered, in the refrigerator until it is firm.

TO ASSEMBLE THE CROUSTADE

Wet a large cookie sheet, shake off the excess moisture, and set aside. Roll the pastry into a 9 x 5-inch rectangle.

Cut the pastry in half lengthwise and transfer one piece to the wet cookie sheet. If you are not using puff pastry, pastry scraps must be docked with a roller docker. Or, lacking a docker, prick the pastry all over with the tines of a dinner fork from one end to the other. This allows steam to escape so the pastry doesn't rise too much.

Place the mushroom mixture down the center of the pastry. There should be a 1-inch border all around the filling.

Brush the border with the beaten egg. Cover with the second piece of pastry, securing its edges to the bottom border. Brush the entire surface with the beaten egg. Place the croustade in the refrigerator to chill and rest for 30 minutes.

---

* One-pound packages of prepared puff pastry can be found in supermarkets and specialty food shops.

PREHEAT THE OVEN TO 400°F

Remove the croustade from the refrigerator and brush it again with the beaten egg. Make two 1-inch round holes, to vent the steam, in the top of the croustade.

Bake on the middle shelf of the oven for 40 minutes, or until the pastry has puffed and its color is a deep, golden brown.

Remove from the oven and, with two metal spatulas, transfer the croustade to a wire rack to cool.

30

CROUSTADE OF CRAB
OR LOBSTER

SERVES 8 TO 10

3 tablespoons unsalted butter
2 tablespoons finely chopped shallots
4 tablespoons all-purpose flour
1 cup milk mixed with ½ cup heavy cream
¾ teaspoon salt
¼ teaspoon freshly ground black pepper
1 teaspoon Dijon mustard
2 tablespoons finely chopped green pepper
2 tablespoons finely chopped red pepper
2 tablespoons dry sherry
1 pound flaked fresh crab or lobster meat

Melt the butter in a heavy skillet, add the shallots, and cook until they are transparent. With a wooden spoon, stir in the flour and cook for a few minutes. With a wire whisk, gradually beat in the milk-cream mixture. Add the salt, pepper, mustard, and red and green peppers. Bring the sauce to a boil, reduce the heat to low, and simmer for 5 minutes. Remove from the heat and stir in the sherry and crab or lobster meat. Scrape the mixture into a large, shallow dish and chill in the refrigerator until firm. Assemble as for the mushroom croustade (page 28).

CELERY VICTOR

This recipe brings me wonderful memories of being a young chef at Chillingsworth on Cape Cod. It's a refreshing first course, particularly good during the warm weather, and it can be made several days before serving.

SERVES 6

3 bunches celery
2 cups fresh Chicken Stock (page 48) or canned broth
1 bay leaf
4 tablespoons white wine vinegar
¾ cup olive oil
½ teaspoon salt
½ teaspoon prepared mustard
12 anchovy fillets, washed under cold running water and patted dry with paper towels
2 large pimientos, cut into long julienne strips
2 hard-cooked eggs, finely chopped
2 tablespoons chopped chives
2 tablespoons chopped parsley

Trim the celery, leaving a heart about 1½ inches wide and 6 inches long. Cut each one in half lengthwise. Place the halves in a large skillet and cover with the chicken stock. Add the bay leaf and bring the stock to a boil, reduce the heat, and simmer, partially covered, for 20 minutes, or until tender. Transfer the celery to a dry platter. Beat the vinegar, oil, salt, and mustard together and pour over the hearts of celery. Cover with plastic wrap and place in the refrigerator to chill.

Garnish the Celery Victor by crisscrossing the anchovies and pimientos on top of the celery hearts. Sprinkle with the chopped egg, chives, and parsley.

CHEESE FONDUE

For 6 or 8 people, Cheese Fondue is not only a pleasant taste treat, it is fun. If you plan to serve it only once in a while, bamboo skewers work just as well as fondue forks.

Be sure to buy a prime quality French or Italian bread. With a fresh green salad, it makes a fine brunch for 4 people.

SERVES 6 TO 8

1 *pound imported Swiss Gruyère cheese*
½ *pound Swiss Emmenthaler cheese*
4 *teaspoons arrowroot*
2 *cups dry white wine*
1 *large garlic clove, peeled and lightly crushed*
3 *tablespoons imported Kirsch*
¼ *teaspoon nutmeg*
⅛ *teaspoon salt*
Freshly ground black pepper to taste
32 *large cubes of Italian bread*

Coarsely grate the Gruyère and Emmenthaler cheeses into a large bowl and toss them together with the arrowroot until they are well combined. Pour the wine into a large enameled casserole, add the garlic, and bring to a boil. Cook the garlic for 2 to 3 minutes and remove with a slotted spoon. Lower the heat to a simmer. Stirring with a wooden spoon, add the cheese mixture one-quarter at a time, letting each addition melt before adding another. When the cheese mixture is smooth, stir in the Kirsch, nutmeg, salt, and pepper to taste.

Place the casserole on top of an electric warming plate. Pass the bread and fondue forks.

$\mathscr{C}$HEESE $\mathscr{S}$OUFFLÉ

When I first started to cook professionally, I was intimidated by soufflé recipes. Read the recipe carefully, be sure your oven registers the correct temperature, and you'll be able to do it without worry.

SERVES 4 TO 6

4 tablespoons butter
4 tablespoons flour
Salt to taste
½ teaspoon cayenne pepper
1½ cups hot milk
6 egg yolks
1 tablespoon softened butter
¾ cup plus 1 tablespoon grated imported Swiss cheese
8 egg whites
¾ cup grated imported Parmesan cheese

PREHEAT THE OVEN TO 400°F

Melt the butter in a medium-sized saucepan over low heat. Gradually add the flour, stirring with a wooden spoon until the mixture is smooth, and cook for 4 to 5 minutes. Remove the saucepan from the heat and add the salt and cayenne pepper. Slowly beat the hot milk into the flour mixture with a wire whisk. Return the saucepan to the heat and bring the sauce to a boil to thicken. Lower the heat and simmer the sauce for a few seconds. Remove from the heat. One at a time, whisk the egg yolks into the sauce and set aside.

Butter the bottom and sides of a 2-quart soufflé dish with the softened butter. Add the 1 tablespoon of Swiss cheese and shake the dish to coat the bottom and sides evenly with the cheese. With a large balloon whisk or an electric mixer beat the egg whites until they form stiff but moist peaks. Stir about one-quarter of the egg whites into the sauce, then scrape the sauce over the remaining egg whites. Mix the remaining Swiss cheese with the

34

Parmesan and sprinkle on top of the sauce. With a large rubber spatula fold all the ingredients together gently but thoroughly. Carefully pour the soufflé mixture into the prepared dish.

Place the soufflé on the middle shelf of the preheated oven and bake for 5 minutes. Reduce the heat to 375°F and continue to bake the soufflé for an additional 20 to 25 minutes, or until the soufflé puffs up 2 to 3 inches above the edge of the dish.

$\mathscr{F}$RIED $\mathscr{C}$HEESE $\mathscr{S}$QUARES

These cheese squares can be served for a first course or shaped into small balls and served with drinks. The basic mixture can be made 2 or 3 days before you shape and fry them.

MAKES 18 SQUARES

6 tablespoons butter
2 cups all-purpose flour
2 cups milk
4 egg yolks
1½ teaspoons salt
⅛ teaspoon cayenne pepper
1½ cups grated imported Swiss cheese
½ cup grated imported Parmesan cheese
3 eggs beaten together with ½ cup milk
2 cups Fresh Bread Crumbs (page 12)
1 quart vegetable oil

In a heavy, medium-sized saucepan, melt the butter over low heat. Gradually stir in 1¼ cups of the flour. Stirring with a wooden spoon until the mixture is smooth, cook for 2 to 3 minutes. Remove the saucepan from the heat and gradually add the milk. Return the saucepan to the heat and bring the sauce to a boil to thicken. Lower the heat and let the sauce simmer for 5 minutes.

Remove the pan from the heat and beat in the egg yolks one at a time. Add the salt, pepper, and grated cheeses, beating the mixture until all the ingredients are well blended.

Spread the mixture on a lightly oiled cookie sheet and, using a metal spatula, shape it into a rectangle or a square. It must be only ½ inch thick. Cover with plastic wrap and place in the refrigerator for 2 to 3 hours or until the cheese mixture is very firm.

With a sharp and lightly oiled knife cut the cheese mixture into

2-inch squares. Dredge each square in the remaining flour and shake off the excess. Using a slotted metal spatula, coat with the beaten egg and milk mixture, then with the bread crumbs.

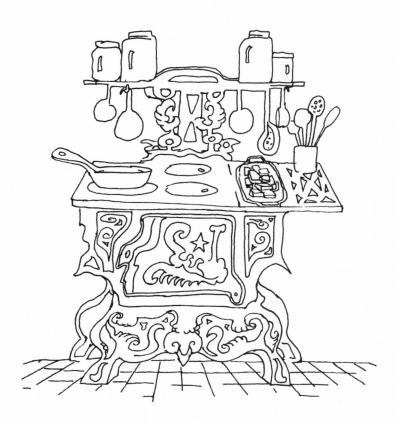

PREHEAT THE OVEN TO WARM

Fill a large cast-iron skillet two-thirds full of vegetable oil. Using a deep-fat-frying thermometer heat the oil to 375°. Gently place the cheese squares in the hot oil 4 to 6 at a time, turning them with a slotted spoon. Fry for 3 to 4 minutes, or until they turn golden brown. Transfer them to a baking sheet lined with paper towels and keep warm in the oven until all the cheese squares are deep-fried.

Liptauer Cheese Spread

This cheese spread is fast and easy to make and everyone loves it. I sometimes add a good splash of Worcestershire sauce. It can also be used as a dip for vegetables by thinning it with a little cream or even milk.

MAKES ABOUT 3 CUPS

1½ cups small-curd cottage cheese
1½ sticks (12 ounces) unsalted butter, softened
2 tablespoons sweet imported Hungarian paprika
½ teaspoon salt
¼ teaspoon white pepper
1 tablespoon crushed caraway seeds
2 teaspoons chopped capers
2 tablespoons grated onion
¾ cup sour cream
¼ cup thinly sliced scallions

With the back of a large wooden spoon, press the cottage cheese through a wire sieve into a medium-sized bowl. Beat in the softened butter, paprika, salt, white pepper, caraway seeds, capers, grated onion, sour cream, and sliced scallions. Refrigerate, covered with plastic wrap, for at least 2 hours before serving.

CHEESE BALLS

Although this recipe makes 36 cheese balls, because of their delicious flavor and light texture don't count on serving more than 8 people.

MAKES ABOUT 3 DOZEN

1½ cups grated Monterey Jack cheese
1½ cups grated sharp cheddar cheese
3 tablespoons all-purpose flour
1½ cups saltine cracker crumbs
4 egg whites
1 tablespoon prepared mustard
Vegetable oil for deep-fat frying
Salt to taste

Mix together the two grated cheeses. Place the flour in a small wire strainer and sieve it over the cheese. Toss the cheeses and flour together. Place the cracker crumbs in a shallow dish (a pie plate works well). Beat the egg whites until stiff and scrape them onto the cheese along with the mustard. Using a large rubber spatula, fold the ingredients together very gently until they are well blended.

Heat the oil in a large cast-iron skillet. Form the mixture into 1-inch balls. Roll the cheese balls in the cracker crumbs and fry them, a few at a time, until they are golden brown.

Drain on paper towels for a few minutes, sprinkle with salt, and serve hot.

*C*HEESE *P*IZZA

From pizza parlors to expensive restaurants serving small pizzas as a first course, the pizza is at the peak of its popularity. Cheese pizza is the basic pizza to which you can add numerous toppings. The best way to learn how to shape the dough is by watching a pizza maker.

MAKES 2 PIZZAS OR SERVES 4

PIZZA DOUGH

1 envelope active dry yeast
¼ teaspoon sugar
1½ cups warm water (110–115°F)
3 cups bread or strudel flour
1½ teaspoons salt
¼ cup olive oil
½ cup cornmeal

PIZZA TOPPING

2 cups Pizza Sauce (page 292)
1 pound grated mozzarella cheese
½ cup olive oil

TO MAKE THE DOUGH

Combine the yeast, sugar, and ¼ cup of the lukewarm water and stir. Set the mixture aside until it doubles in volume.

Place 2½ cups of the flour, the salt, and the olive oil in a large bowl. Pour in the yeast mixture and the remaining water. Stir with a wooden spoon until the flour has absorbed all of the liquid.

With your hands, turn the dough out onto a clean, lightly floured surface. Knead the dough for 10 minutes. If it sticks to the surface, add more

40

flour until the dough no longer sticks to your hands or the board as you knead it. Place the dough in a bowl and cover with a towel. After 1½ hours the dough should be double in volume. To test whether the dough has risen enough, press two fingertips into the surface. If the indentations remain, it is ready. Divide the dough in half, shape it into two balls, and let rest for 15 minutes.

TO SHAPE THE DOUGH

Place one ball of dough on a work surface lightly dusted with the cornmeal. Flatten the ball with the palms of your hands. Keep slapping the dough with your palms and every so often give it a quarter of a turn to ensure a round disk. With your thumb and forefinger pinch the edge of the dough to create a small lip or rim, which will help to contain the sauce. Continue to slap and stretch the dough until you have a 20-inch pizza shell.

TO ASSEMBLE THE PIZZA

PREHEAT THE OVEN TO 500°F

Ladle 1 cup of sauce on top of the pizza shell and swirl it around until it coats the surface evenly. Sprinkle with half of the cheese and dribble half of the olive oil on top.

Bake the pizza on the lowest shelf of the preheated oven for 30 to 40 minutes, or until the cheese and sauce are bubbling and the edges of the dough are a dark brown.

While the first pizza is baking there is ample time to shape the second. If a second pizza is not needed, all the ingredients can be frozen for another time.

CHEESE AND GREEN CHILI DIP

Serve this with raw vegetables or deep-fried tortilla chips.

MAKES 3 CUPS

3 tablespoons butter
3 tablespoons all-purpose flour
1½ cups light cream
4 medium-sized ripe tomatoes, blanched, peeled, seeded, and chopped
½ teaspoon finely chopped garlic
¾ teaspoon salt
One 4-ounce can green chilies, drained, seeded, and coarsely chopped
2½ cups grated Monterey Jack cheese

Melt the butter in a heavy 1½-quart saucepan, stir in the flour, and cook for 2 minutes. Gradually whisk in the cream and bring the mixture to a boil to thicken; reduce the heat and cook for 3 minutes. Remove from the heat and set aside.

Combine the tomatoes, garlic, and salt in a heavy saucepan and cook over high heat, stirring constantly, until the water is cooked out of the tomatoes. Reduce the heat to low and stir in the cream sauce and green chilies. Then gradually add the grated cheese. Pour the mixture into a chafing dish to keep warm.

Soups

*F*ISH *S*TOCK

You may use flounder or sole or the bones and heads of any white-fleshed fish. Whatever you use, you must wash the heads and bones under cold running water to free them of any blood. Fish stock may be stored in the refrigerator for several days or frozen for up to 3 months.

MAKES ABOUT 6 CUPS

2 *pounds heads and bones from white-fleshed fish*
½ *cup dry white wine*
½ *cup chopped celery, with some leaves*
1 *cup chopped onion*
1 *bay leaf*
¼ *teaspoon thyme*
½ *teaspoon salt*
3 *white peppercorns, crushed*

Wash the fish heads and bones under cold running water, place them in a large pot, and cover with cold water. Bring the liquid to a simmer and cook for 5 minutes. With a slotted spoon, skim off the foam as it rises to the top of the pot. Add the wine, celery, onion, bay leaf, thyme, salt, and peppercorns. Continue to simmer the stock for 30 minutes.

Strain the stock through à fine sieve lined with cheesecloth into a larger bowl.

45

BEEF STOCK

This recipe requires 3 pounds of short ribs, so you might want to plan on serving the ribs for a dinner. If you do, try the Mustard Sauce on page 289 or the Salsa Cruda on page 288.

MAKES ABOUT 3 QUARTS

3½ pounds beef shin bones, sawed into 1½-to-2-inch lengths
3 pounds beef short ribs
2 pounds veal shank, sawed into 1½-to-2-inch lengths
3 pounds beef bones, sawed into small pieces
2 large leeks
2 large carrots, scraped and sliced thick
2 large stalks of celery with leaves
2 medium-sized yellow onions, skins left on but washed
3 sprigs parsley
1 bay leaf
½ teaspoon thyme
1 clove
2 teaspoons salt
8 whole black peppercorns

Place the shin bones, short ribs, veal shank, and beef bones in a very large pot. Add 6 quarts of cold water. The contents of the pot should be covered by at least 2 inches of water. If not, add more water.

Very slowly bring the water to a simmer, skimming off the foam that forms with a slotted spoon. *Do not let the water come to a boil.* Simmer for 45 minutes.

Remove the roots and all but 2 inches of the green from the leeks. Cut the leeks crosswise and place them in a large wire strainer. Hold the leeks under cold running water to remove any sand. Add the leeks, carrots, celery, onions, parsley, bay leaf, thyme, clove, salt, and pepper to the stock. Partially cover the pot and simmer for 6 hours.

Remove from the heat and let the stock cool to room temperature. Remove the short ribs and reserve. Remove the bones and discard them. Strain the stock through a wire strainer lined with a double thickness of damp cheesecloth into a large container. Discard the vegetables.

Refrigerate the stock until the fat solidifies on top. Before using the stock, remove the fat.

Beef stock can be stored in the refrigerator for 3 to 4 days or frozen for up to 3 months.

CHICKEN STOCK

If you have the freezer space, by all means make 6 quarts of stock. After chilling and removing the fat, store in 1-pint containers in the freezer, where it will keep safely for 8 to 12 weeks. If storage is a problem, the recipe can be cut in half, but you should plan to have chicken soup that day to use the additional 4 pieces of stewing chicken.

MAKES ABOUT 6 QUARTS

1 *large stewing chicken cut into 8 pieces plus 5 pounds backs and necks or chicken wings, or a combination of both*
2 *large leeks*
2 *large carrots, scraped and sliced thick*
2 *large stalks of celery with leaves*
2 *medium-sized onions, peeled*
3 *sprigs of parsley*
1 *bay leaf*
½ *teaspoon thyme*
1 *clove*
2 *teaspoons salt*
8 *whole black peppercorns*

Place the cut-up chicken and the chicken parts in a large pot. Add 6 quarts of cold water. The chicken should be covered by at least 2 inches of water. If not, add more water.

Very slowly bring the water to a simmer, skimming off the foam that forms with a slotted spoon. *Do not let the water come to a boil.* Simmer the chicken for 45 minutes. Remove the roots and all but 2 inches of the green leaves from the leeks. Cut the leeks crosswise, place them in a large wire strainer, and hold under cold running water to remove any sand. Add the cleaned leeks, carrots, celery, onions, parsley, bay leaf, thyme, clove, salt, and pepper to the stock. Partially cover the pot and simmer for 2 hours. Turn off the heat and let the stock cool to room temperature.

48

Remove the chicken and chicken parts. Strain the stock through a wire strainer lined with a double thickness of damp cheesecloth into a container. Discard the vegetables.

Refrigerate the stock until the fat solidifies on top. Before using the stock, remove the fat.

ℱLEMISH ℭREAM OF ℭHICKEN ℒOUP

This soup calls for veal bones and 1½ pounds of lean shin of beef. Both of these ingredients are used to intensify the broth. Cold beef salad can be made with the shin; or freeze it in the reserved stock and use it another time to make beef vegetable soup. Actually you will be cooking two recipes at one time.

SERVES 8

1½ pounds lean beef shin
1 pound veal bones, cut into 1-inch pieces
4 quarts fresh Chicken Stock (page 48)
2 large onions, grated
2 celery stalks with leaves
1 large leek, cut into rounds and rinsed under cold running water
1 large carrot
2 sprigs curly parsley
One 5-pound roasting chicken, quartered
4 egg yolks beaten with 1 cup heavy cream
Fresh lemon juice to taste
White pepper to taste

Place the beef shin, veal bones, and chicken stock in an 8-quart soup pot. Bring the stock to a boil over high heat. Add the onions, celery, leek, carrot, and parsley. Skim off the foam as it rises to the surface. Add the chicken and again skim off the foam. Reduce the heat to low and simmer partially covered for 1 hour.

Continue to simmer the soup for an additional 1½ hours or until the chicken is tender.

Remove the chicken and beef and set them aside.

Strain the remaining contents of the pot into a large, heavy casserole. Discard the veal bones and vegetables. With a ladle skim off the fat from the surface. Remove 4 cups of the stock and set aside.*

When the chicken is cool enough to handle, remove the skin and bones and discard them. Cut the chicken pieces into 2 x ½-inch slices and return to the broth in the casserole. Bring to a rolling boil; reduce the heat to a simmer. Beat ½ cup of the hot broth into the egg and cream mixture and slowly whisk it into the broth. Remove from the heat and add the lemon juice. Add white pepper to taste. Serve immediately.

* Dice the beef and add it to the 4 cups of reserved stock. Freeze for later use as is or add cooked vegetables or noodles.

CHILLED CREAM OF CAVIAR SOUP

When John Clancy's restaurant in New York City was reviewed by the New York Times *restaurant reviewer, Mimi Sheraton, she wrote: "The cold cream of caviar soup sounded dreadful, but tasted wonderful, with its underplaying of chives, modifying the gentle fishiness of red caviar."*

SERVES 6 TO 8

3 large leeks
1½ pounds potatoes, peeled and sliced ⅓ inch thick
1 large onion, sliced
2 quarts fresh Chicken Stock (page 48) or canned broth
1 cup heavy cream
Salt and freshly ground white pepper to taste
12 tablespoons caviar
2 tablespoons chopped parsley

Remove the roots and all but 2 inches of the green from the leeks. Cut the leeks crosswise and place them in a large wire strainer. Hold the leeks under cold running water to remove any sand. Place the leeks, potatoes, onion, and chicken stock in an 8- or 10-quart casserole. Bring the stock to a boil, reduce heat to a simmer, and cook partially covered for 45 to 50 minutes, or until the vegetables are very soft.

Force the soup through a food mill or purée it in a food processor. Return it to the casserole, add the cream, and taste for salt and pepper. Let the soup simmer for an additional 5 minutes.

Allow the soup to cool, then refrigerate it until it is very cold. Just before serving, stir in the caviar and the chopped parsley.

CLAM AND TOMATO SOUP

Ask your fish store for the smallest littlenecks. Sometimes they try to sell you topnecks, which are just a little smaller than cherrystones.

SERVES 4 TO 6

6 tablespoons olive oil
1½ teaspoons finely chopped garlic
½ cup finely chopped onion
¾ cup dry white wine
4 cups canned plum tomatoes, drained of liquid and coarsely chopped
½ teaspoon oregano
3 dozen littleneck clams, scrubbed
1½ cups water
Salt and freshly ground black pepper to taste
4 tablespoons flat-leaf parsley, chopped

Heat the olive oil in a heavy 3- or 4-quart saucepan and cook the garlic and onion until the onion is transparent. Pour in the wine and cook to reduce by half. Add the tomatoes and the oregano and simmer for 10 minutes.

Put the clams in a large skillet, hinge side down, add the water, and cook, covered, over high heat for 8 to 10 minutes, or until the clams open. Discard any unopened clams. With a slotted spoon, transfer the clams in their shells to large soup plates, dividing them equally. If the liquid in the skillet looks a bit sandy, strain it through a sieve lined with a double thickness of cheesecloth into the soup base.

Return the soup to a boil, taste for salt and pepper, and ladle over the clams. Sprinkle with the chopped parsley and serve at once.

$\mathscr{L}$OBSTER $\mathscr{B}$ISQUE

My customers enjoy gallons of this bisque every week. For my taste, Lobster Bisque is the king of all bisques.

SERVES 6

Two 2-pound live lobsters
4 tablespoons butter
½ cup finely chopped celery, including leaves
½ cup finely chopped onion
¼ cup chopped carrots
¼ teaspoon thyme
1 teaspoon dried tarragon
1 bay leaf
⅛ teaspoon cayenne pepper
½ cup cognac or brandy
1½ cups dry white wine
6 cups fresh Chicken Stock (page 48) or canned chicken broth
⅓ cup uncooked rice
1½ cups canned Italian plum tomatoes with their liquid
4 teaspoons tomato paste
¾ cup heavy cream

Plunge the tip of a sharp, heavy knife just behind the eyes of each lobster. Cook the lobsters in enough boiling water to cover for 3 minutes. Remove them to a colander to drain. When the lobsters are cool enough to handle, twist off the claws and the tails, extract the meat, and set aside. With a heavy cleaver chop the shells and the bodies.

Heat the butter in a large, shallow saucepan. Add the celery, onion, carrots, thyme, tarragon, bay leaf, and cayenne. Cook until the vegetables are lightly colored.

Stir in the lobster shells. Pour in the cognac or brandy and ignite. Add the white wine and stock, the rice, tomatoes, and tomato paste. Bring

54

the liquid to a boil, reduce the heat to a simmer, and cook partially covered for 40 minutes.

Purée the bisque through a food mill into a large bowl and return it to the saucepan. Cut the lobster meat into a small dice and add to the bisque. With a wire whisk, gradually beat in the heavy cream. Bring the bisque to a simmer and serve in warm soup plates.

*O*YSTER *S*TEW

Do not consider trying to make this stew in advance and reheat it later. It must be prepared quickly and served immediately, or the oysters will toughen.

SERVES 4 TO 6

3 cups shucked oysters, with their liquor
3 cups light cream
8 tablespoons butter, cut into equal-sized pieces
1/4 teaspoon thyme
1 teaspoon Worcestershire sauce
Salt and freshly ground black pepper to taste
Imported sweet Hungarian paprika

Place a wire strainer over a 1-quart saucepan, add the oysters, and allow their liquor to drain. Remove the oysters and set aside. Add the light cream to the oyster liquor and heat to serving temperature.

Heat 2 tablespoons of the butter in a large skillet. Add the oysters and cook them for a minute or two, or until the edges start to curl. Pour in the cream mixture. Add the thyme, Worcestershire sauce, and salt and pepper to taste.

Serve in heated soup bowls with one pat of the remaining butter added to each bowl and a dusting of paprika.

*O*YSTER *S*OUP

If you plan to prepare Oyster Soup several hours before serving, stop after the soup has simmered for a few minutes. Just before serving, add the remaining ingredients. Please don't substitute curly parsley for flat-leaf parsley because the soup will not have the flavor it's meant to have.

SERVES 4 TO 6

2½ cups shucked oysters and their liquor
Fresh Chicken Stock (page 48) or canned broth
3 tablespoons butter
½ cup very finely chopped celery
½ cup finely chopped scallions
3 tablespoons flour
½ teaspoon salt
⅛ teaspoon cayenne pepper
3 egg yolks
¼ cup chopped flat-leaf parsley

Place the oysters in a sieve over a bowl and drain. Measure the oyster liquor and add enough chicken stock to make 3 cups.

Melt the butter in a 3- or 4-quart saucepan over low heat. Add the celery and scallions and, stirring with a wooden spoon, cook the vegetables for about 5 minutes. Add the flour and mix well. Remove from the heat.

Stirring with a wire whisk, pour in the oyster–chicken stock mixture in a slow stream and cook over high heat until the liquid comes to a boil. Reduce the heat to low, add the salt and pepper, and simmer for a few minutes. (The recipe may be prepared in advance to this point.)

Beat the egg yolks in a small bowl, add ¼ cup of the hot liquid, and mix with the yolks. Now, add the oysters and pour the yolk mixture into the soup. Cook an additional few minutes until the soup thickens slightly. Do not allow the soup to come to a boil or it will curdle.

Serve the oyster soup in heated soup bowls and garnish with the chopped parsley.

$\mathscr{S}$EA $\mathscr{S}$CALLOP $\mathscr{C}$HOWDER

Sometimes sea scallops can be giant in size; if this is the case, cut them in half before slicing them.

SERVES 6 TO 8

6 *tablespoons butter*
2 *large onions, coarsely chopped*
6 *cups half and half*
2 *medium-sized potatoes, peeled and cut into small dice*
1½ *pounds fresh sea scallops*
Salt and freshly ground black pepper to taste

Heat 4 tablespoons of the butter in a large saucepan, add the onions, and cook them until soft. Add the half and half and let it simmer for about 20 minutes.

Cook the potatoes until tender in enough salted water to cover, about 6 to 8 minutes. Strain the water off and set the potatoes aside.

Strain the half and half mixture through a fine sieve and discard the onions. Wash and dry the pot and place on medium heat.

Heat the remaining 2 tablespoons of butter, add the sliced scallops, and cook, stirring frequently, until they turn opaque.

Pour the half and half mixture into the scallop pot and add the diced potatoes. Reheat and taste for salt and pepper.

BEEF BROTH WITH MARROW AND CHIVES

In general, canned beef broth or dehydrated packaged stock bases are not the best substitutes for the real thing. If for some reason you have to resort to canned broth, use only 2 cups of it and make the difference up with 4 cups of chicken broth. Combine both broths in a 2-quart saucepan, add a little chopped onion or scallion and some celery leaves, and simmer for 20 minutes. Strain and proceed with the recipe.

SERVES 4 TO 6

4 pieces of beef marrow bones, at room temperature
2 tablespoons chopped chives
3 tablespoons dry sherry
6 cups fresh Beef Stock (page 46)

With the handle of a wooden spoon, push the marrow from the bones. With a paring knife, gently scrape the marrow to remove any splinters. Slice the marrow in thin rounds, about ⅛ inch thick, and set aside.

Just before serving, divide the marrow, chives, and sherry among the soup plates. Bring the beef stock to a boil and immediately ladle the hot broth into the soup plates and serve.

German Vegetable Beef Soup

This is actually a winter vegetable soup. If you wish, you can add ½ cup of cooked peas and 2 large tomatoes, blanched, peeled, seeded, and cut into half-inch slices.

SERVES 6

1½ pounds boneless beef chuck, cut into 1-inch cubes
1½ pounds beef marrow bones, sawed into 1-inch pieces
2 whole peeled onions
2 cloves
1 bay leaf
1½ teaspoons salt
6 peppercorns
2 leeks
1 medium celery root, peeled and diced
1 medium carrot, peeled and diced
2 medium potatoes, peeled and diced
1 small parsnip, peeled and diced
2 tablespoons chopped parsley

Place the beef chuck and marrow bones in a large pot. Add 3 quarts cold water. The contents of the pot should be covered by at least 2 inches of water. If not, add more water.

Very slowly bring the water to a boil, skimming off the foam that forms with a slotted spoon. Reduce the heat to a simmer and add the onions, cloves, bay leaf, salt, and peppercorns. Simmer the broth for 2 hours partially covered. Remove and discard the onions and bay leaf. Transfer the bones to a bowl and allow to cool. Remove the roots and all but 2 inches of the green from the leeks. Cut them crosswise, place in a large wire strainer, and hold under cold running water to remove any sand.

When the bones are cool enough to handle, scoop out the marrow and add it to the soup along with the leeks, celery root, carrot, potatoes, and parsnip. Continue to simmer the soup for 30 minutes, or until the vegetables are tender.

Serve the soup in heated plates, garnished with a little chopped parsley.

OXTAIL SOUP

A cold winter's afternoon is the time to enjoy this rich, full-bodied soup.

SERVES 6

4 tablespoons Clarified Butter (page 283)
3 pounds oxtails, disjointed
1 large onion, sliced
1 medium-sized carrot, coarsely chopped
1 cup celery, diced
9 cups fresh Chicken Stock (page 48) or canned broth
6 peppercorns
3 sprigs parsley
1 bay leaf
1 large tomato, coarsely chopped
1 teaspoon dried thyme
Salt and freshly ground black pepper to taste
½ cup diced carrot
½ cup diced celery
½ cup diced white turnip
Chopped parsley, for garnish

In a large, heavy soup pot heat the butter, add the oxtails, and cook, turning the pieces until they are brown. Add the onion, carrot, and celery and cook until they are lightly browned. Add the chicken stock, peppercorns, parsley, bay leaf, tomato, and thyme. Bring the stock to a boil, reduce the heat, and cook partially covered for 3½ to 4 hours, or until the meat is tender. Remove the oxtails from the soup with a slotted spoon and set aside.

Strain the soup through a fine sieve into a large heat-proof bowl, taste for salt and pepper, and return the broth to the soup pot along with the diced carrot, celery, and white turnip. Simmer the soup for 20 minutes, or until the vegetables are tender. Skim off any surface fat and return the oxtails to the pot.

Serve in heated soup platters, garnished with chopped parsley.

*E*SCAROLE *S*OUP

Keep this recipe in mind when time is running short. There is no other soup that gives such great pleasure from so little effort.

SERVES 6 TO 8

8 cups fresh Chicken Stock (page 48) or canned broth
1 large head escarole
Salt and freshly ground black pepper to taste
½ cup freshly grated imported Parmesan cheese

Place the chicken stock in a 3- or 4-quart saucepan and bring it to a boil over high heat. Reduce the heat to a simmer.

Remove the root end of the escarole and discard. Chop the escarole coarsely and place in a large wire strainer. Hold the chopped escarole under cold running water to remove any grit.

Stir the escarole into the simmering stock. Simmer until the escarole is completely wilted, about 5 minutes. Depending upon the stock used, the soup may need salt and pepper.

Serve in heated soup plates and pass the Parmesan cheese separately.

CREAM OF CAULIFLOWER SOUP

By replacing the cauliflower with broccoli and following the same instructions you can make a perfectly good cream of broccoli soup.

SERVES 6

2 pounds cauliflower
3 cups fresh Chicken Stock (page 48) or canned broth
3 cups water
6 tablespoons butter
1/2 cup finely chopped onion
1/2 cup all-purpose flour
1 cup milk
1 1/2 teaspoons salt (depending on broth)
1/4 teaspoon nutmeg
2 egg yolks
1 teaspoon lemon juice

With a sharp knife, cut away the base of the cauliflower and remove any green leaves. Gently separate the cauliflower into florets and place them in a bowl of cold water.

Combine the chicken stock and water in a large saucepan and bring to a boil over high heat. Drop in the florets and allow the liquid to return to the boil; cook for 8 minutes. Turn off the heat and remove the florets with a slotted spoon or a skimmer and set aside to cool.

Melt the butter in a large, heavy saucepan over low heat. Add the onion and cook until transparent. Gradually add the flour, stirring with a wooden spoon until the mixture is smooth. Cook for 2 to 3 minutes. Remove the saucepan from the heat and slowly add the broth and milk. Return the saucepan to the heat and bring the sauce to a boil to thicken slightly. In the meantime, coarsely chop all but six of the florets. Add the chopped cauliflower to the simmering soup along with the salt and nutmeg. Lower the heat and let the soup simmer for 20 minutes. Strain the soup through a sieve into a bowl.

With the back of a wooden spoon purée the cauliflower through the sieve. Return the soup to the saucepan. Beat the egg yolks in a small bowl with a fork. Add ½ cup of the soup, then whisk the egg mixture into the saucepan and cook over low heat for 2 minutes.

Place one whole floret in each heated soup plate. Add the lemon juice and ladle the soup into the plates.

COLD CUCUMBER SOUP

This is truly a hot weather soup and very refreshing. Try it "on the rocks."

SERVES 6 TO 8

3 *medium-sized firm cucumbers*
6 *cups plain yogurt*
2 *tablespoons distilled white vinegar*
2 *tablespoons chopped fresh mint*
2 *teaspoons chopped fresh dill*
2½ *teaspoons salt*

Scrape the peel from the cucumbers and slice them in half lengthwise. With a small spoon scrape out the seeds and discard them.

In a large mixing bowl, beat the yogurt with a wire whisk until it is smooth. Add the vinegar, mint, dill, and salt. Coarsely grate the cucumbers into the yogurt mixture. Stir all the ingredients until well blended.

Cover with plastic wrap and chill in the refrigerator for about 2 hours before serving.

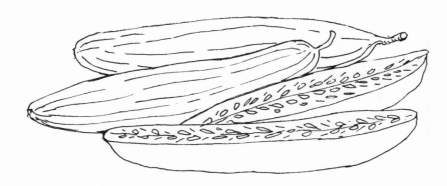

CREAM OF
WATERCRESS SOUP

Cream of Watercress Soup can also be served chilled. If you are using rich homemade stock, the soup will thicken when chilled, and you may have to add a bit more heavy cream to thin it.

SERVES 4 TO 6

4 *tablespoons butter*
¼ *cup finely chopped onion*
3 *large bunches watercress, coarsely chopped*
½ *teaspoon salt*
¼ *teaspoon white pepper*
4 *tablespoons all-purpose flour*
6 *cups fresh Chicken Stock (page 48) or canned broth*
2 *egg yolks beaten with ½ cup heavy cream*

Melt the butter in a 2½- or 3-quart heavy saucepan. Add the onion and cook until transparent. Stir in the watercress, salt, and pepper and cook, stirring, until the watercress has wilted. Stir in the flour and cook for 2 minutes.

Scrape the contents of the pan into the container of a food processor. Purée the mixture (you may have to add a little chicken stock). Return it to the saucepan and add the chicken stock. Simmer the soup for 10 minutes, then taste for seasoning.

Mix a little hot soup into the egg yolk–cream mixture. Then gently stir it back into the soup and cook over very low heat for 1 minute. Taste for seasoning and serve in heated soup plates.

Chilled Green Pea Soup with Mint

This soup is truly suitable for hot weather. It could be served at an elegant garden wedding or put in a thermos and taken on a picnic or to the beach.

SERVES 6 TO 8

8 cups fresh Chicken Stock (page 48) or canned broth
4 cups fresh or frozen peas
1½ cups chopped onion
½ cup chopped celery
¼ teaspoon ground cloves
1 cup chopped fresh mint
1 cup heavy cream
Salt and freshly ground black pepper to taste
Fresh mint leaves for garnish

In a 3½- or 4-quart casserole, combine the chicken stock, peas, onion, celery, ground cloves, and chopped mint. Bring the mixture to a boil, reduce the heat to simmer, and cook, partially covered, for 45 minutes. Purée the soup in the container of a food processor. Return it to the casserole, whisk in the heavy cream, and bring to a boil. Taste for salt and pepper. Pour the soup into a storage container and let it cool to room temperature. Place it in the refrigerator to chill.

Serve in chilled soup plates and garnish with fresh mint leaves.

ℙOTATO AND
ℂUCUMBER ℒOUP

This is one of those soups that can be enjoyed hot or chilled. When serving it cold, I mix 2 tablespoons of fresh, chopped dill into 1 cup of yogurt and place a dollop on each serving.

SERVES 6 TO 8

3 medium-sized cucumbers
6 boiling potatoes (about 2 pounds)
1 medium-sized onion, peeled and sliced
1½ teaspoons salt
Freshly ground white pepper to taste
1 cup heavy cream
2 cups milk
2 tablespoons chopped fresh dill

Peel and seed the cucumbers and set one aside. Coarsely chop 2 cucumbers and set aside. Peel the potatoes and cut them into large dice. Place the chopped cucumbers, diced potatoes, and sliced onion in a medium-sized saucepan. Cover with cold water, add the salt, and bring the water to a boil. Reduce to a simmer and cook until the potatoes are soft. Strain the liquid into a large bowl and purée the solids in a food processor. Return the liquid and the puréed vegetables to the saucepan. Add the ground white pepper, heavy cream, and milk, and simmer for about 5 minutes.

Cut the remaining cucumber in very thin slices and reserve.

Just before serving, taste for seasoning and stir in the sliced cucumber and chopped dill.

*G*AZPACHO

This soup of Spanish peasant origin now graces many of the best dining tables around the world. Here in the United States, I think, every cook adds his or her own signature to gazpacho. If you wish you can chop an additional amount of any of the vegetables in the recipe and use them as a garnish.

SERVES 4 TO 6

1 *large cucumber, peeled and chopped*
4 *large ripe tomatoes, blanched, peeled, seeded, and chopped*
1 *large onion, chopped*
1 *green pepper, cut in half, deribbed and chopped*
1½ *teaspoons finely chopped garlic*
Three 1-inch-thick slices of French or Italian bread
3 *cups cold water*
3 *tablespoons red wine vinegar*
3 *teaspoons salt*
3 *tablespoons olive oil*

Combine the chopped cucumber, tomatoes, onion, green pepper, and garlic in a large bowl. A few handfuls at a time, place the vegetables in the container of a food processor and purée. Trim the crusts from the bread and process the bread with some of the vegetable purée. Add the cold water, vinegar, salt, and olive oil. Taste for salt; you may want to add a bit more. Cover with plastic wrap and chill for about 2 hours before serving.

CORN CHOWDER

Don't feel that you are cheating if you use frozen corn kernels; they make just as good a chowder as fresh. To make Oyster Corn Chowder, simply cook 24 oysters in some of their liquor. Place 3 oysters in each soup plate and add the liquor to the chowder. Ladle the hot chowder over the cooked oysters and serve immediately.

SERVES 6 TO 8

3 cups fresh or frozen corn kernels
¼ pound lean salt pork
2 cups finely chopped onion
4 medium-sized boiling potatoes cut into ½-inch dice
3 cups water
2 cups milk
1 cup heavy cream
Salt and freshly ground black pepper to taste

Purée half of the corn in a food processor. Remove the rind from the salt pork and discard. Dice the salt pork and render it in a 4- or 6-quart pot or casserole until crisp and brown. Remove the salt pork and set aside.

Add the chopped onion to the pot and sauté it in the pork fat until light golden brown. Stir in the corn purée and the remaining corn kernels, the diced potatoes, and the water. Bring the mixture to a boil and then reduce to a simmer. Partially cover the pot and cook the mixture until the potatoes are tender. Add the milk, cream, and reserved pork bits. Bring the chowder to a boil, taste for salt and pepper, and serve.

BEAN AND PASTA SOUP

To eliminate the first step, you can soak the beans in 1 quart of cold water overnight. Because soups freeze well, I always make more than I need. If you need only 4 to 6 servings, make the full recipe and freeze the remainder.

SERVES 6 TO 8

1½ *cups navy beans*
¼ *cup vegetable or olive oil*
1 *cup finely chopped onion*
¼ *cup finely chopped celery*
1 *teaspoon finely chopped garlic*
2 *cups diced smoked ham*
3 *quarts fresh Chicken Stock (page 48) or canned broth*
1 *teaspoon salt*
Freshly ground black pepper to taste
1 *cup spaghetti, broken into small pieces*
½ *cup freshly grated imported Parmesan cheese*

Place the navy beans in a large pot and cover with cold water. Bring the water to a rolling boil. Remove from the heat, cover the pot, and let the beans soak for 1 hour. Then drain the beans and discard the water.

Heat the oil in a large pot and cook the onion, celery, and garlic until the onion is soft but not brown. Stir in the ham, add the beans, chicken stock, salt, and pepper. Bring to a boil, reduce the heat to a simmer, and cook the soup partially covered for about 2 hours.

Place half the beans in the container of a food processor and purée. Stir the purée into the soup.

Add the spaghetti and cook for 12 minutes, or until tender. Taste for salt and pepper. Serve with grated Parmesan cheese passed separately at the table.

POULTRY

RUSSIAN CHICKEN CUTLETS

These cutlets can be shaped the day before and stored, covered with plastic wrap, in the refrigerator. If you like, you may use half ground veal and half chicken.

SERVES 4 TO 6

6 *slices white bread trimmed of crusts*
6 *tablespoons milk*
2 *pounds boned and skinned chicken breasts*
8 *tablespoons softened butter*
¾ *teaspoon salt*
⅛ *teaspoon cayenne pepper*
1½ *cups Fresh Bread Crumbs (page 12)*
1½ *cups Clarified Butter (page 283)*

Break the slices of bread into small pieces and place them in a bowl. Sprinkle them with the milk and set aside. Cut the chicken breasts into small pieces and place them in the container of a food processor. Process the chicken until it becomes a smooth paste. Squeeze the excess milk from the bread pieces, add the bread to the chicken, and process again until the mixture is smooth. Now add the butter, salt, and cayenne pepper and process again until all the ingredients are well blended.

Remove the mixture to a flat plate and chill in the refrigerator for 20 minutes.

Dip your hands in cold water (to keep the mixture from sticking) and shape the mixture into 6 oval patties about 4½ to 5 inches long. Completely coat the patties with bread crumbs.

Fry the cutlets in the clarified butter in a large sauté pan for about 5 minutes on each side, or until the crumb coating is golden brown.

Sprinkle a little of the hot butter from the pan over each cutlet.

CHICKEN BREASTS WITH HAM AND CHEESE

This dish can be prepared many hours before cooking. Simply place the casserole in the oven 6 to 8 minutes before serving time.

SERVES 6

Three 1-pound chicken breasts, boned, skinned, and halved
Salt and freshly ground black pepper to taste
1 cup flour
6 tablespoons butter
4 tablespoons vegetable oil
6 slices Smithfield ham
6 thin slices Monterey Jack cheese
1 tablespoon grated imported Parmesan cheese ⎫
1 tablespoon Fresh Bread Crumbs (page 12) ⎬ *mixed together*
2 teaspoons chopped parsley ⎭

PREHEAT THE OVEN TO 450°F

With a sharp knife slice each half chicken breast in half again horizontally. Season the chicken breasts lightly with salt and pepper. Gently pound each breast between two pieces of waxed paper until they are of even thickness, then dip them in the flour and shake off any excess.

Heat the butter and oil in a large, heavy skillet until very hot. Sauté the breasts quickly until they are a light golden brown. Using tongs, transfer the breasts to a plate.

Lightly butter a large, shallow ovenproof dish. Place six pieces of chicken breast in the dish, then place a slice of ham and a slice of cheese on top of each piece. Top the ham and cheese with the remaining chicken. Sprinkle the chicken with the bread crumb mixture. Dribble 1 teaspoon of the fat in the skillet on top.

Bake the chicken, uncovered, on the middle shelf of the oven for 6 to 8 minutes. Serve immediately.

CHICKEN STEW WITH GREEN TOMATOES

When you make the trip to the Spanish or Mexican specialty store to buy the green tomatoes, get some fresh tortillas to serve with the stew.

SERVES 6

3 tablespoons butter plus 2 tablespoons vegetable oil
3 pounds boneless, skinless chicken breast cut into 1½-inch pieces
Salt and freshly ground black pepper to taste
¾ cup chopped onion
½ teaspoon finely chopped garlic
2 cups fresh Chicken Stock (page 48) or canned broth
One 10-ounce can green tomatoes
One 4-ounce can green chilies, stemmed, seeded, and coarsely chopped
½ teaspoon dried thyme
½ teaspoon dried marjoram

Heat the butter and oil in a large, heavy skillet. Toss the chicken with salt and pepper and cook over high heat, stirring constantly, until the pieces are lightly brown in color. (Do not overcook the chicken pieces; they should be raw inside.) Transfer the chicken pieces to a medium-sized flame-proof casserole.

Add the onion and garlic to the fat remaining in the skillet and cook until the onion is transparent. Pour in the chicken stock, tomatoes, chilies, thyme, and marjoram. Cook over medium heat, stirring and crushing the tomatoes with a large metal spoon, for about 15 minutes. Add the chicken pieces and cook for 2 to 3 minutes. Taste for salt and pepper and serve with boiled rice.

FRIED CHICKEN

Unfortunately, about 10 years ago the Coach House restaurant in New York City stopped serving fried chicken. It was unfortunate because it was the best fried chicken I have ever tasted. You can re-create this wonderful chicken at home by using canned lard instead of the kind that comes packaged like butter.

SERVES 4

One 2½-to-3-pound frying chicken
2 teaspoons salt
½ teaspoon ground black pepper } *mixed together*
2 eggs, lightly beaten
¾ cup milk } *mixed together*
1½ cups flour
3½ to 4 pounds canned lard

Disjoint the chicken to make 8 pieces: 2 wings, 2 thighs, 2 drumsticks, and 2 breasts. Sprinkle the pieces with the salt and pepper mixture.

Dip the chicken in the egg-milk mixture, then dredge it in the flour until all the pieces are well coated. Place the chicken on a jelly roll pan and allow it to sit for 1 hour. Melt the lard in a large cast-iron skillet over low heat; it should be 2½ inches deep. Increase the heat and bring the temperature of the lard to 375°F (use a deep-fat-frying thermometer). With metal tongs, gently lower 3 or 4 pieces of chicken into the hot lard. Turning them often, fry until they are golden brown. As they brown, transfer them to a large plate lined with paper towels. Continue frying the chicken, keeping in mind that the dark meat will take 10 to 12 minutes and the white meat about 8 to 10.

ℭHICKEN IN ℒEMON ℐELLY

This chicken recipe can be made 2 days in advance. It is truly a great summer dish.

SERVES 4

½ cup olive oil
One 3-to-3½-pound frying chicken, cut into 8 pieces
Salt and freshly ground black pepper to taste
½ cup thinly sliced onion
½ cup thinly sliced carrots
½ cup thinly sliced celery
3 cloves bruised garlic
1 cup dry white wine
1 cup white wine vinegar
1 cup fresh Chicken Stock (page 48) or canned broth
2 whole cloves
1 bay leaf
¼ teaspoon thyme
1 lemon cut lengthwise then crosswise into ⅛-inch slices

Heat the olive oil in a large skillet. Season the chicken pieces with a little salt and pepper, then brown them in the oil and place them in a 4- or 6-quart casserole. Add the sliced onion, carrots, celery, and garlic. Pour in the white wine, vinegar, and chicken stock, then add the cloves, bay leaf, and thyme.

Bring the liquid to a boil, reduce the heat to simmer, and cook the chicken for 45 minutes. Remove from the heat and allow the chicken to cool in the casserole.

Arrange the cooked chicken in a large, deep serving dish, pour the remaining contents of the casserole over it, and float the lemon slices on top. Cover with plastic wrap and refrigerate for 4 to 6 hours or until the liquid turns to jelly.

Chicken Breasts Milanaise Style

The same bread crumb mixture works as well on veal chops as on chicken breasts. After the chicken breasts are coated with the bread crumb mixture they may be stored in the refrigerator for several hours.

SERVES 4

Four 8-ounce chicken breasts, boned and skinned
Salt and freshly ground black pepper
1 cup flour
2 eggs
1¼ cups Fresh Bread Crumbs (page 12)
¾ cup freshly grated Parmesan cheese
½ teaspoon crumbled oregano
¼ cup chopped flat-leaf parsley
½ cup Clarified Butter (page 283)
4 lemon wedges

Place the chicken breasts on a large sheet of wax paper. Season them lightly with salt and pepper. Place a second piece of wax paper on top of the breasts and with the flat side of a cleaver, gently pound the breasts until they are about ⅓ inch thick.

You will need three soup plates or any shallow dishes similar in size. Place the flour in one, beat the eggs in another, and mix the bread crumbs, cheese, oregano, and parsley in the third. One at a time, dredge the chicken breasts first in the flour, then in the beaten egg, and then coat them evenly on both sides with the bread crumb mixture.

Heat the clarified butter in a heavy 12-inch skillet until very hot. Add the chicken breasts and sauté them on both sides for a total of about 3½ to 4 minutes, or until firm to the touch and golden brown in color.

Place on individual serving plates and garnish with the lemon wedges.

Chicken Hash Cakes

This is also a great way to use up leftover turkey. I sometimes top the hash cakes with a poached egg.

SERVES 6

HASH CAKES

- ½ pound boiling potatoes
- 4 tablespoons butter, cut into small pieces
- 3 cups coarsely chopped cooked chicken
- ¾ cup chopped onion
- ½ cup finely chopped celery
- ¼ cup chopped green pepper
- ¼ cup chopped parsley
- 1 egg
- ⅓ cup heavy cream
- 2 teaspoons salt
- ¼ teaspoon cayenne pepper

COATING

- 1 cup all-purpose flour
- 3 beaten eggs mixed with ½ cup milk
- 2 cups Fresh Bread Crumbs (page 12)
- 1½ cups Clarified Butter (page 283)

TO MAKE THE HASH CAKES

Cook the potatoes in enough boiling water to cover for 20 minutes. Drain the potatoes and when they are cool enough to handle peel them and cut them into small pieces. In a large mixing bowl, combine the potatoes, butter, cooked chicken, onion, celery, green pepper, parsley, egg, heavy cream, salt, and cayenne pepper. Mix thoroughly with your hands. In two batches, grind the mixture in a food processor until it is smooth enough to hold its shape. If it crumbles, add a little more cream or an additional egg yolk.

Divide the chicken hash into 12 equal portions and shape into cakes about ¾ inch thick and 3 inches in diameter. Place the cakes on a wax-paper-lined jelly roll pan and chill for 30 minutes.

One at a time, dredge the hash cakes in the flour, dip them in the egg-milk mixture, then coat them with the bread crumbs. Return the hash cakes to the refrigerator for 20 minutes.

TO FRY THE HASH CAKES
PREHEAT THE OVEN TO THE LOWEST TEMPERATURE

Heat half of the clarified butter in a large skillet until very hot. Fry 6 hash cakes at a time for 3 to 4 minutes on each side, or until they are golden brown. Transfer the cakes to a jelly roll pan and put them in the preheated oven. Discard the butter in the skillet and wipe it clean with paper towels. Cook the remaining cakes in the same fashion using the remaining clarified butter.

ᴹOCK ꟻRIED ᶜHICKEN ᴮREASTS

After these poached chicken breasts are covered with the chopped walnuts, they will look like fried chicken. They are a nice addition to a cold buffet—or take them on a picnic.

SERVES 6

CHICKEN BREASTS

Six 8-ounce chicken breasts, boned with skin left on
1 cup thinly sliced onion
½ cup chopped celery with some leaves
2 teaspoons salt

TOPPING

1 cup softened cream cheese
½ cup fresh Mayonnaise (page 294)
3 tablespoons chopped chives
½ teaspoon salt
¼ teaspoon freshly ground white pepper
1 teaspoon grated lemon rind
1½ cups chopped walnuts

TO PREPARE THE CHICKEN

Place the chicken, skin side up, in one layer in a 12-inch skillet. Add the onion, celery, and salt. Pour enough water in the skillet to cover the chicken breasts by 1 inch. Bring the liquid to a boil, reduce to simmer, and cook for 8 to 10 minutes, or until the flesh feels firm to the touch. Remove from the heat and let the chicken cool to room temperature. Drain the chicken, remove the skin, and immediately wrap the pieces in plastic wrap and refrigerate.

TO PREPARE THE TOPPING

Combine the cream cheese, mayonnaise, chives, salt, pepper, and lemon rind in a small bowl and cream until they are well blended and the mixture is very smooth.

Remove the chicken breasts from the refrigerator and with a metal icing spatula spread the cream cheese mixture on them. Gently press the chicken in the chopped walnuts so they adhere, completely covering the cream cheese mixture. Refrigerate until ready to serve.

*C*HICKEN AND *S*HRIMP *C*ASSEROLE

Although this recipe calls for 1 cup of diced Serrano ham, which you will find in any Spanish specialty food shop, you can substitute Smithfield ham or prosciutto.

SERVES 4

One 2½-to-3-pound frying chicken, cut into 8 pieces
½ teaspoon salt
¼ teaspoon freshly ground black pepper
½ cup Clarified Butter (page 283)
1 cup chopped onions
1 teaspoon chopped garlic
3 tablespoons all-purpose flour
1 cup diced Serrano ham
½ cup dry white wine
1 cup fresh Chicken Stock (page 48) or canned broth
12 medium-sized shrimp, peeled and deveined
12 black olives
2 tablespoons finely chopped flat-leaf parsley

Pat the chicken pieces dry with paper towels and season with salt and pepper.

Heat the clarified butter in a heavy 12-inch skillet. Add the chicken, skin side down, and cook for 4 to 6 minutes on each side, or until it is golden brown. Transfer the pieces as they brown to a 3- or 4-quart casserole.

Discard all but 4 tablespoons of the butter from the skillet, add the onions, and cook them, stirring, until they turn light brown. Add the garlic and cook for a few minutes longer. With a wooden spoon, stir the flour into the onion mixture. Add the ham, white wine, and chicken stock. Bring the liquid to a boil, scraping up any brown bits that cling to the bottom and sides of the pan. When the sauce has thickened slightly, pour it over the chicken. Bring the sauce in the casserole to a boil and cook the chicken, partially covered, for 30 minutes. Drop in the shrimp and black olives and cook 3 to 4 minutes, or until the shrimp turn pink. Test the chicken for doneness by piercing the thigh with the tip of a paring knife. If the juices run clear the chicken is done.

Arrange the chicken on a large, heated serving platter. Using a slotted spoon, remove the shrimp and olives from the casserole and scatter them over the chicken. Taste the sauce for seasoning, then spoon it over the chicken. Garnish with the chopped parsley.

ROILED KEWERED

HICKEN INGS

The wing is my favorite part of the chicken. For quite a few years of my life you could get the wings only if you bought the whole chicken. Now almost any butcher and all supermarkets sell chicken parts. Skewered and broiled fresh vegetables such as tomatoes, eggplant, and green peppers go well with the chicken wings.

SERVES 4

3½ pounds chicken wings
1 large onion, peeled
2 teaspoons salt
½ cup fresh lemon juice
¼ teaspoon ground saffron mixed with ¾ cup yogurt

Put the chicken wings in a large bowl. Grate the onion into the bowl and add the salt and lemon juice. Toss the chicken wings with your hands to coat them evenly with the marinade. Cover with plastic wrap and let them marinate for 2 hours at room temperature.

Light a 2-to-3-inch-thick layer of mesquite or charcoal in a grill. When the coals burn white the temperature will be proper for cooking. String the chicken wings on 18-inch steel skewers, penetrating through the first and second joints of each wing. Pushing them close together you should get 8 wings to a skewer.

Broil the chicken wings about 4 inches from the coals for about 10 to 12 minutes, turning the skewers and basting them with the saffron-yogurt mixture every 3 to 4 minutes.

If you get rained out, you can easily do this in the oven broiler; they will take 4 to 6 minutes longer to cook.

RY

CHICKEN BREASTS PAPRIKA

The 4½ teaspoons of flour beaten into the sour cream keep the cream from curdling. This same process works for any sauce calling for sour cream.

SERVES 4

Four 8-ounce chicken breasts, boned with skin left on
½ teaspoon salt
½ cup Clarified Butter (page 283)
1 cup very finely chopped onion
½ teaspoon chopped garlic
4½ teaspoons imported sweet Hungarian paprika
1 cup fresh Chicken Stock (page 48) or canned broth
1½ cups sour cream
4½ teaspoons all-purpose flour
3 large sprigs parsley

Pat the chicken breasts dry with paper towels and season them with salt. Heat the clarified butter in a heavy 12-inch skillet until very hot. Add the chicken breasts, skin side down, and cook for about 4 minutes, or until golden brown. Remove the chicken to a plate.

Pour off all but 2 tablespoons of the butter and cook the onion until it is nicely browned. Add the garlic and cook for 1 minute longer. Stir in the paprika, add the chicken stock, and bring to a boil. Reduce the heat to simmer and return the chicken breasts to the skillet. Cover the skillet and simmer the chicken breasts for 4 to 6 minutes, or until they feel slightly springy to the touch. Remove the chicken from the skillet.

Place the sour cream in a small bowl and beat in the flour with a wire whisk. Whisk the sour cream into the liquid in the skillet and bring to a boil. Return the chicken breasts to the skillet and cook for 2 minutes longer.

Arrange the chicken breasts on a heated platter and pour the sauce over them. Garnish with the sprigs of parsley.

*O*NE-*P*OT
*C*HICKEN *D*INNER

For a little extra color I sometimes cook 1½ cups of green peas and sprinkle them on the other vegetables just before serving.

SERVES 4

One 3-pound roasting chicken
Salt and freshly ground black pepper to taste
½ teaspoon dried thyme
2 garlic cloves, crushed
1 large onion, peeled and quartered
¼ pound salt pork
1 tablespoon Clarified Butter (page 283)
16 small white onions, peeled
8 small carrots, scraped
2 small bay leaves
16 small new potatoes, peeled and set aside in cold water

PREHEAT THE OVEN TO 350°F

Season the chicken with the salt, pepper, and thyme. Stuff the cavity with the garlic and onion and truss the chicken.

Blanch the salt pork in boiling water for 5 minutes. Remove from the water and when it is cool enough to handle, pat it dry with paper towels and cut into ¼-inch dice.

Melt the butter in a heavy 12-inch skillet. Add the diced salt pork and render it until it is brown and crisp, then remove with a slotted spoon to paper towels to drain.

Brown the chicken on all sides in the rendered pork fat. Remove the chicken to a large, heavy casserole. Cook the onions and carrots in the remaining fat until lightly colored. Season the vegetables with a little salt

90

and pepper and add them to the casserole with the 2 bay leaves. Cover the casserole with a tight-fitting lid and place on the middle shelf of the pre-heated oven to bake for 45 minutes. Remove the cover and baste the chicken with the juices at the bottom of the casserole.

Drain the potatoes and add them to the casserole. Replace the lid and cook for an additional 30 minutes. Test the chicken for doneness by inserting the tip of a small paring knife in a thigh. If the juices run clear the chicken is done. If not, continue to cook the chicken for 5 to 10 minutes longer.

Place the chicken on a large heated platter, remove the trussing string, and display the vegetables attractively around the chicken.

$\mathscr{P}$OACHED $\mathscr{C}$HICKEN IN A $\mathscr{C}$REAMY $\mathscr{G}$ARLIC $\mathscr{S}$AUCE

Steamed new potatoes, asparagus, and dark pumpernickel go well with this chicken dish. Don't be afraid of all that garlic. It's wonderful poached!

SERVES 6 TO 8

CHICKEN

One 4½-to-5-pound roasting chicken, quartered
2½ quarts fresh Chicken Stock (page 48) or canned broth
18 to 24 large cloves of garlic, peeled and tied in a small piece of cheesecloth

SAUCE

3 tablespoons butter
4 tablespoons all-purpose flour
4 cups fresh Chicken Stock (page 48) or canned broth
3 egg yolks
¾ cup heavy cream
1 tablespoon fresh lemon juice

TO PREPARE THE CHICKEN

Place the chicken in a 6- or 8-quart casserole. Pour in the chicken stock. If the stock does not cover the chicken by 2 inches, add more stock or water. Add the sack of garlic, bring the liquid to a boil, lower the heat, and simmer, partially covered, for 1½ hours. Test the chicken for doneness by piercing the thigh with the tip of a paring knife. If the juices run clear the chicken is done.

Remove the casserole from the heat. Remove the cheesecloth sack and purée the garlic through a wire strainer into a small bowl with the back of a wooden spoon and set aside.

TO MAKE THE SAUCE

Melt the butter in a heavy 1½- or 2-quart saucepan. Stir in the flour and cook for 2 minutes. Whisk in the stock and the reserved puréed garlic. Bring the mixture to a boil, reduce the heat to low, and simmer for 5 minutes.

Whisk the egg yolks and the cream together in a small bowl, then beat in about ½ cup of the hot sauce. Pour the cream mixture back into the sauce, whisking constantly. Add the lemon juice. Cook for 2 minutes and remove the sauce from the heat.

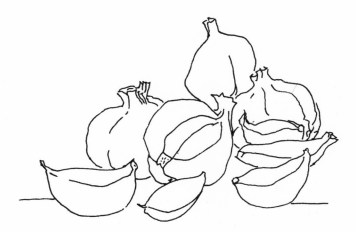

TO ASSEMBLE THE POACHED CHICKEN

Remove the chicken from the casserole and place it on a large, heated platter. Remove the skin from the chicken and discard. Cut the chicken into serving pieces and blot the platter with paper towels to remove any juices. Spoon some of the sauce over the chicken and serve the remaining sauce in a sauce boat.

CREAMED CHICKEN AND CHIPPED BEEF ON CORNBREAD WEDGES

This recipe is a takeoff on an old railroad luncheon dish. When I served brunch in my restaurant, I adapted it for the menu. I'm sure you will like it as much as my customers did.

SERVES 6 TO 8

CHICKEN

4 tablespoons Clarified Butter (page 283)
Four 8-ounce chicken breasts, boned and skinned
1/4 teaspoon salt

SAUCE

3 tablespoons butter
4 tablespoons all-purpose flour
4 cups fresh Chicken Stock (page 48) or canned broth
3 egg yolks
3/4 cup heavy cream
1 tablespoon fresh lemon juice
2 tablespoons chopped chives

FINISHING

One 3 1/2 ounce jar of chipped beef, cut into julienne strips
1 Skillet Cornbread (page 308), cut into 8 wedges

TO PREPARE THE CHICKEN

Melt the butter in a heavy 12-inch skillet over low heat. Season the chicken breasts with the salt and with a pair of tongs bathe the chicken in the butter. Place a tight-fitting lid on the skillet and cook the chicken over low heat for 6 minutes. Remove the chicken breasts to a plate to cool.

TO MAKE THE SAUCE

Melt the butter in a 2- or 2½-quart saucepan. Stir in the flour and cook for 2 minutes. Whisk in the chicken stock and bring the mixture to a boil. Reduce the heat to low and simmer for 5 minutes. Whisk the egg yolks with the cream in a small bowl and beat in about ½ cup of the hot sauce. Pour the cream mixture back into the sauce, whisking constantly. Cook the sauce for 2 minutes, remove from the heat, and stir in the lemon juice and the chopped chives.

TO ASSEMBLE THE DISH

Cut the cooked chicken breasts into 1-inch cubes and add to the sauce along with the chipped beef. Reheat the mixture over low heat until the chicken is hot. Place wedges of warm cornbread on individual serving plates and ladle the chicken-beef mixture on top. Serve immediately.

95

$\mathscr{C}$HICKEN $\mathscr{F}$RICASSEE

Most people prefer to remove the skin from the chicken, but do as you wish. You might like to serve Potato Dumplings (page 218) with the fricassee.

SERVES 4 TO 6

CHICKEN

One 3½-pound chicken, cut into 8 pieces
3 cups fresh Chicken Stock (page 48) or canned broth
1 large onion, peeled and sliced
1 carrot, scrubbed and cut into chunks

SAUCE

3 tablespoons butter
3 tablespoons all-purpose flour
2 cups fresh Chicken Stock (page 48) or canned broth
2 egg yolks
¼ cup heavy cream
1 teaspoon fresh lemon juice
Salt and freshly ground black pepper to taste
1 tablespoon chopped parsley

TO PREPARE THE CHICKEN

Place the chicken in a large casserole and add the stock. Bring the stock to a simmer and, with a slotted spoon, remove the foam as it rises to the top. Add the onion and carrot and simmer for about 35 minutes, or until the chicken is tender. Test by inserting the tip of a paring knife into the thigh. If the juices run clear the chicken is done.

Using tongs, transfer the chicken to a heated serving platter and cover it with foil to keep it warm.

TO MAKE THE SAUCE

Melt the butter in a heavy 1-quart saucepan over medium heat. When the butter is melted, stir in the flour and cook for 2 minutes. Whisk in the stock and let it come to a boil to thicken. Reduce the heat to low and simmer for 5 minutes. Beat the egg yolks and heavy cream together. Add a little of the hot sauce to the cream mixture. Whisk the mixture into the sauce and let it cook for 2 minutes. Do not allow it to come to a boil or it may curdle. Add the lemon juice, taste for salt and pepper, and pour over the chicken. Sprinkle with the chopped parsley and serve immediately.

Chicken in Green Tomato Sauce

Many supermarkets now have Spanish and Mexican food sections where you can find green tomatoes.

This dish can be made the day before and reheated gently over low heat. It doesn't matter whether the chicken waits for the sauce or the sauce waits for the chicken.

Plain boiled rice is a nice accompaniment.

SERVES 4

CHICKEN

One 3½-pound frying chicken, cut into 8 pieces
1 cup fresh Chicken Stock (page 48) or canned broth

SAUCE

½ cup shelled pumpkin seeds
⅓ cup shelled walnuts
⅓ cup blanched almonds
1 cup fresh Chicken Stock (page 48) or canned broth
1 large green pepper
One 10-ounce can green tomatoes
1 cup chopped onion
¼ cup chopped cilantro
1 teaspoon Tabasco sauce
½ teaspoon finely chopped garlic

Salt and freshly ground black pepper to taste

TO PREPARE THE CHICKEN

Place the chicken pieces in a large, shallow pot. Add enough water just to cover the chicken. Add the salt and bring to a boil; reduce the heat and simmer for 20 minutes. Remove from the heat and allow the chicken to cool in its liquid to room temperature.

When the chicken is cool enough to handle, remove the skin and discard.

Set the chicken aside until the sauce is made.

TO MAKE THE SAUCE

Combine the pumpkin seeds, walnuts, and almonds in the container of a food processor. Process the seeds and nuts until they just turn into a paste. Gradually add the chicken stock. Scrape the mixture into a fine strainer set over a bowl and with a wooden spoon force the mixture through. Set aside.

Cut the green pepper in half, remove the ribs and seeds, and chop it coarse. Combine the green pepper, canned green tomatoes, chopped onion, cilantro, Tabasco sauce, and garlic in the container of a food processor. Process the ingredients until they turn into a purée.

Add the nut mixture and continue to process until all the ingredients are well blended.

Pour the sauce into a 10- or 12-inch skillet. Add the chicken and cook for about 10 minutes, or until the chicken is heated through. Arrange the chicken on a heated platter and pour the sauce over it. Serve immediately.

*C*HICKEN *B*REASTS *H*OLLANDAISE

This chicken breast recipe can be served for a late brunch or for lunch, but it is equally good for dinner. Try serving it on fried toast and garnished with broccoli.

SERVES 4

4 tablespoons Clarified Butter (page 283)
Four 8-ounce chicken breasts, boned and skinned
1/4 teaspoon salt
2 tablespoons chopped shallots
1/4 cup dry sherry
1 1/4 cups heavy cream
4 slices Westphalian ham, cut into julienne strips
1/2 recipe Hollandaise Sauce (page 293)

Melt the butter in a heavy 12-inch skillet over low heat. Season the chicken breasts with the salt and with a pair of tongs bathe the chicken breasts in the butter. Place a tight-fitting lid on the skillet and cook the chicken over low heat for 8 minutes, or until there is a slight springiness to the touch. Remove the chicken breasts to a warm platter.

Add the shallots and cook for a few seconds, then pour in the sherry and heavy cream. Reduce the mixture by half over high heat, stir in the ham, remove from the heat, and beat in the hollandaise sauce. Taste for seasoning, spoon the sauce over the chicken breasts, and serve.

$\mathscr{B}$ROILED $\mathscr{D}$EVILED $\mathscr{C}$HICKEN

This recipe also works well with 4 fresh Cornish game hens substituted for the chicken.

SERVES 4

6 tablespoons melted butter
4 tablespoons olive oil
¼ teaspoon cayenne pepper
1 teaspoon salt
One 2½-to-3-pound chicken, neck and backbone removed, quartered
⅓ cup finely chopped shallots
3 tablespoons chopped flat-leaf parsley
¼ cup dry vermouth

PREHEAT THE BROILER

Combine the melted butter, olive oil, cayenne pepper, and salt in a small bowl. Brush both sides of the chicken with the butter-oil mixture, arrange the chicken, skin side down, on a broiler pan, and place about 4 inches from the heat. Broil for 10 minutes, then turn the chicken pieces and brush again with the butter-oil mixture. Continue to broil for an additional 10 minutes.

Add the shallots and parsley to the remaining butter-oil mixture. Test the chicken for doneness by piercing the thickest part of the thigh with the tip of a paring knife. If the juices run clear the chicken is done; if not broil for another 2 to 3 minutes. When the chicken is done, remove it to a serving platter and keep warm.

Remove the rack from the broiler pan and add the dry vermouth. With a metal spatula scrape the brown bits from the bottom of the pan. Add the shallots and parsley, mix well, then pour the sauce over the chicken and serve.

ℒEMON ℰHICKEN

There are two additional ways you can proceed with this recipe. For pungency, stir ¼ cup chopped cilantro into the sauce just before serving, or stir in ¼ cup finely chopped mint. Boiled rice is a nice accompaniment for the chicken.

SERVES 4

One 2½-to-3-pound frying chicken, cut into 8 pieces
1 teaspoon salt
Freshly ground black pepper to taste
6 tablespoons olive oil
1 cup finely chopped onion
1 teaspoon finely chopped garlic
1 tablespoon sweet imported Hungarian paprika
½ teaspoon ground ginger
½ teaspoon turmeric
1 cup fresh Chicken Stock (page 48) or canned broth
2 large lemons, thinly sliced
16 small whole green olives

Season the chicken pieces with the salt and pepper. Heat the olive oil in a heavy 12-inch skillet and add the chicken, skin side down, a few pieces at a time. Cook the chicken for 4 to 6 minutes on each side, or until it is golden brown. As they brown, transfer the chicken pieces to a 3- or 4-quart casserole.

Discard all but 2 tablespoons of the oil from the skillet. Add the onion and cook until it is brown; add the garlic and cook for 1 minute longer. Stir in the paprika, ginger, and turmeric. Pour in the chicken stock, bring to a boil, and pour the contents of the skillet over the chicken. Return the liquid to a boil, reduce the heat, and simmer, covered, for 30 minutes. Test the chicken for doneness by piercing the thigh with the tip of a paring knife. If the juices run clear the chicken is done.

102

Transfer the chicken to a large, heated platter, add the lemon slices and the olives to the sauce in the pan, bring to a boil, and remove from the heat. Taste for seasoning and spoon the sauce over the chicken.

COUNTRY CAPTAIN CHICKEN

In many books this chicken is known as East Indian Chicken Curry. Country Captain dates back many years. It is an elegant dish for a dinner party. My rendition includes orzo, a noodle of Greek origin (available in most markets), boiled, drained, and tossed with a little butter, salt, and pepper as a unique accompaniment to the Country Captain Chicken.

SERVES 4

One 2½-to-3-pound frying chicken, cut into 8 pieces
Salt and freshly ground black pepper to taste
½ cup Clarified Butter (page 283)
1½ cups all-purpose flour
½ cup finely chopped onion
¼ cup diced green pepper
½ teaspoon finely chopped garlic
¼ teaspoon thyme
2 teaspoons curry powder
½ cup dry white wine
¼ cup currants
2 cups canned tomatoes, drained, seeded, and chopped
½ cup whole almonds, toasted and coarsely chopped

Season the chicken pieces with a little salt and pepper. Heat the butter in a heavy 12-inch skillet. Dredge the chicken pieces in the flour and brown them on all sides in the hot butter. Remove the chicken to a plate and set aside.

Add the onion, green pepper, garlic, thyme, and curry powder to the skillet and cook until the onion is brown. Add the white wine and scrape the pan with a metal spatula to loosen any brown bits from the bottom and sides.

104

Return the chicken pieces to the skillet and add the currants and tomatoes. Cover the pan and cook over low heat for 20 minutes, or until the chicken is tender.

Place the cooked chicken on a heated platter, pour the sauce over it, sprinkle with the chopped almonds, and serve.

CHICKEN SAUTÉ WITH ONIONS AND POTATOES

After the onions, potatoes, and chicken have been browned, you may stop at that point and continue with the recipe 40 minutes before you wish to serve it.

SERVES 4

12 tablespoons Clarified Butter (page 283)
16 small white onions, peeled
16 small new potatoes, peeled and shaped to the size of the onions
One 3½-pound chicken, cut into 8 pieces
½ teaspoon salt
Freshly ground black pepper to taste
1½ cups Basic Brown Sauce (page 287)
1 bunch watercress, cleaned

In a large, heavy skillet heat 3 tablespoons of the butter until it is very hot. Add the onions and toss them around by shaking the skillet until they are golden brown on all sides. With a slotted spoon remove the onions to a plate and set aside.

Discard any butter from the skillet and carefully wipe it clean with paper towels. Add to the skillet an additional 3 tablespoons of the butter. Heat the butter until it is very hot. Add the potatoes and brown them exactly like the onions. Remove the potatoes from the skillet with a slotted spoon and add them to the onions. Clean the skillet and set aside.

Season the chicken pieces with the salt and pepper. Heat 3 more tablespoons of the butter in the skillet until it is very hot and brown half of the chicken skin side down. When the chicken is brown, transfer it to a plate. In the same manner, using a clean skillet, brown the remaining chicken in the last 3 tablespoons of butter.

Turn the chicken skin side up and return the chicken from the plate to the skillet also, skin side up. Scatter the onions and potatoes over the chicken. Cover the skillet and cook for 30 minutes.

Remove the chicken, potatoes, and onions to a large serving dish and discard any fat from the skillet. Pour the brown sauce into the skillet and with a metal spatula scrape all the browned particles from the bottom and sides of the pan. Taste for seasoning and spoon the sauce over the chicken. Garnish with the watercress.

Marinated Broiled Duck

If you wish to get a head start, marinate the ducks the day before and keep them in the refrigerator until you broil them. I enjoy serving Green Rice (page 258) with the ducks.

SERVES 4

Two 5-pound ducks, cut into quarters
1 cup vegetable oil
¾ cup sherry wine vinegar
1½ teaspoons salt
Freshly ground black pepper to taste
1 cup sliced onion
3 large garlic cloves, crushed
2 bay leaves, crumbled
2 teaspoons ground ginger

With sharp scissors, cut away all exposed fat from the duck pieces. Wash the pieces under cold running water and pat dry with paper towels. Place the duck in a large shallow bowl. Add the oil, sherry wine vinegar, salt, pepper, sliced onion, crushed garlic, crumbled bay leaves, and ground ginger. Toss the duck pieces around until they are well coated with the marinade.

Allow the duck to marinate for 4 hours at room temperature. Every so often, baste the pieces with the marinade.

PREHEAT THE BROILER

Remove the pieces of duck from the marinade and pat them dry with paper towels. Strain the marinade into a measuring cup and discard the vegetables.

Arrange the duck pieces skin side down on the broiler rack. Broil them about 4 inches from the heat for 30 minutes. As the ducks broil, baste them with the strained marinade every 10 minutes. Turn the pieces over and continue to baste and broil for an additional 15 to 20 minutes, until the duck is tender and deep brown. Arrange the pieces attractively on a large, heated serving platter.

$\mathscr{B}$RAISED $\mathscr{S}$TUFFED $\mathscr{Q}$UAIL

Braised Stuffed Quail, served with the Potatoes Parisienne on page 223, or the Potato Dumplings on page 218, and a green vegetable, makes a wonderful dinner for company.

SERVES 4

STUFFING

1½ *pounds sausage meat*
½ *cup finely chopped onion*
1 *teaspoon finely chopped garlic*
1½ *cups dried bread crumbs*
¼ *cup finely chopped parsley*
Salt and freshly ground black pepper to taste

QUAIL

8 *oven-ready quail*
¾ *teaspoon salt*
½ *teaspoon freshly ground black pepper*
½ *cup Clarified Butter (page 283)*
½ *cup finely chopped onion*
4 *tablespoons all-purpose flour*
1 *cup dry Marsala wine*
3 *cups fresh Chicken Stock (page 48) or canned broth*

TO MAKE THE STUFFING

Cook the sausage meat in a heavy 10- or 12-inch skillet over very low heat, stirring every few minutes, until it loses its raw color. With a slotted spoon, remove the meat to a medium-sized bowl. Pour off all but 2 tablespoons of the fat that has collected in the skillet. Add the onion and garlic

110

and cook until the onion is transparent. Scrape the contents of the skillet on top of the cooked sausage meat. Add the dried bread crumbs and chopped parsley and with a wooden spoon mix until well blended. Taste for salt and pepper and allow the mixture to cool to room temperature.

TO PREPARE AND STUFF THE QUAIL

Wash the quail under cold running water inside and out and pat them dry with paper towels. Season the cavities with the salt and pepper. Stuff the quail with the pork mixture and truss them with small trussing skewers.

Heat the clarified butter in a heavy 12-inch skillet until very hot, add the birds, and brown them on all sides, turning them frequently. When they are browned, transfer them to a 4- or 6-quart casserole.

Pour off all but 2 tablespoons of the fat from the skillet. Add the onion and cook until it is golden brown. Mix in the flour and cook for a few minutes. Stir in the Marsala wine and the chicken stock. Bring the liquid to a boil over high heat, scraping up the brown bits that cling to the bottom and sides of the skillet. Pour the mixture over the quail and return the liquid to a boil. Reduce the heat to simmer, cover the casserole, and cook for about 30 minutes. Insert the tip of a paring knife into the thigh; if the juices run clear the quail are done, if not cook for 5 to 10 minutes longer.

Arrange the quail on a heated serving platter and spoon the sauce over them.

ℱROGS ℒEGS ℐAKITORI ℐTYLE

Using fresh frogs legs from France marinated in a Japanese sauce, put on bamboo skewers from Taiwan, grilled over American mesquite, and brushed with a teriyaki glaze makes this the most international dish ever served at Clancy's restaurant.

SERVES 6

MARINADE

½ cup fresh Chicken Stock (page 48) or canned broth
½ cup sherry
2 tablespoons Japanese soy sauce
3 teaspoons sugar
1 tablespoon grated fresh ginger root

Approximately 48 frogs legs (depending upon size)
12 scallions, cut into 1-inch pieces

TERIYAKI GLAZE

½ cup marinade
4 teaspoons sugar
1 tablespoon cornstarch mixed with 4 teaspoons water

TO MAKE THE MARINADE

Combine the chicken stock, sherry, soy sauce, sugar, and grated ginger root. Add the frogs legs and marinate in the refrigerator for about 2 hours.

TO GLAZE AND GRILL THE FROGS LEGS

Combine the marinade with the sugar in a small saucepan and heat over a low flame. Stir in the cornstarch mixture and cook, stirring constantly, until it thickens into a glaze.

Remove the frogs legs from the remaining marinade and string them alternately with the scallions on skewers. Grill over the coals or in the oven broiler, basting with the teriyaki glaze, for 4 to 6 minutes depending upon their size.

MEATS

$\mathscr{S}$HELL $\mathscr{S}$TEAKS IN A $\mathscr{C}$OGNAC $\mathscr{S}$AUCE

If it's available, and if you wish, you may substitute crème frâiche for the heavy cream to make a richer sauce.

SERVES 4

Four 8-ounce boneless shell steaks, 1 inch thick, fat removed
4 teaspoons salt mixed with 1 tablespoon freshly ground black pepper
4 tablespoons Clarified Butter (page 283)
¼ cup cognac
1½ cups Basic Brown Sauce (page 287)
¼ cup heavy cream

Rub the salt and pepper mixture on both sides of the shell steaks. Heat the clarified butter in a large, heavy skillet until it is very hot. Place the steaks in the skillet and cook them for 4 minutes on each side for rare or 6 minutes on each side for medium rare, or to your guests' tastes. Remove the steaks to a heated platter. Pour off any fat in the pan, add the cognac, and ignite it with a match. When the flame subsides, add the brown sauce and cream, stir together, and bring to a boil. Taste for seasoning and pour over the steaks.

$\mathscr{F}$ILET $\mathscr{M}$IGNON $\mathscr{E}$SZTERHÁZY

This famous Austrian dish is usually made with a whole roasted filet with the sauce poured over it. Using individual filets makes it easy to serve and you can cook the filets to individual taste.

SERVES 4

SAUCE

3 tablespoons butter
1 cup finely chopped onion
½ teaspoon finely chopped garlic
¼ cup finely chopped carrots
3 tablespoons all-purpose flour
2⅓ cups fresh Beef Stock (page 46) or canned chicken broth
3 whole allspice, crushed
2 bay leaves
4 peppercorns, crushed
¼ teaspoon dried thyme
One ½-inch strip lemon peel
3 slices lean bacon, sliced crosswise into ⅛-inch pieces
3 tablespoons white wine vinegar
¾ cup heavy cream
2 teaspoons fresh lemon juice

GARNISH

1 large parsnip, scraped
1 medium-sized carrot, scraped
1 rib of celery, scraped
3 sour gherkin pickles

Four 8-ounce filets mignons
Salt and freshly ground black pepper
4 tablespoons Clarified Butter (page 283)

TO MAKE THE SAUCE

Heat the 3 tablespoons butter in a medium-sized saucepan. Add the onion, garlic, and carrots. Cook the vegetables until they are lightly colored. Stir the flour into the vegetables and when the flour is completely absorbed, gradually add the beef stock.

Over high heat bring the liquid to a boil to thicken. Reduce the heat to simmer and add the allspice, bay leaves, crushed peppercorns, thyme, lemon peel, bacon, and white wine vinegar. Partially cover the pan and simmer for 45 minutes. Then strain the sauce through a sieve into a small saucepan. Beat in the heavy cream and lemon juice, reheat the sauce, and keep warm.

TO PREPARE THE GARNISH

Cut the vegetables into a 3 x ¼-inch julienne strips. Cook all but the gherkins in lightly salted water for 3 to 4 minutes, or until tender. Drain the vegetables in a small sieve, then place them on paper towels and toss with the gherkins.

TO PREPARE THE FILLETS

Pat the filets dry with paper towels and season them lightly with salt and pepper. Heat the clarified butter in a heavy skillet until it is very hot. Sauté the filets in the butter, 4 minutes on each side for rare.

Transfer the filet mignons to a heated platter. Spoon some sauce over the meat and garnish with the pickles and julienned vegetables. Serve the remaining sauce in a sauce boat.

*P*ICADILLO

This makes a great filling for omelets, or use it as a filling for green peppers.

SERVES 4 TO 6

6 tablespoons vegetable oil
1 tablespoon annatto seeds
2½ pounds ground chuck
1 tablespoon salt
1½ cups finely chopped onion
1½ teaspoons finely chopped garlic
3 large green bell peppers, seeded and finely chopped
1 teaspoon dried red pepper flakes
2½ cups canned tomatoes, drained and chopped
½ teaspoon ground cloves
¼ teaspoon ground cinnamon
½ cup small pimiento-stuffed olives
⅔ cup seedless raisins
¼ cup white distilled vinegar

In a large, heavy skillet heat the vegetable oil with the annatto seeds over low heat. Stirring the seeds, cook for 6 to 8 minutes. Remove the seeds with a slotted spoon and discard. Add the ground chuck, stirring to break up lumps. Cook the beef until it shows no sign of pink, then stir in the salt, onion, garlic, and green pepper and cook for 6 to 8 minutes. Add the dried red pepper flakes, tomatoes, ground cloves, cinnamon, olives, and raisins. Simmer, uncovered, for 15 minutes. Just before serving stir in the white vinegar.

$\mathscr{H}$AMBURGERS OR $\mathscr{H}$AMBURGER $\mathscr{S}$TEAKS

For my taste, the best hamburger is made with a combination of chuck and shin of beef. I'm much against adding any seasoning to the chopped meat.

The meat should be shaped with a very light hand and broiled to one's taste. The fun comes with the many toppings. My preference is a thick slice of onion and a little catsup or mustard, although many people like sliced tomato, lettuce, and mayonnaise. Garnishes for hamburger could go on and on.

The hamburger bun should be toasted and brushed with melted butter.

MAKES FOUR 8-OUNCE HAMBURGER STEAKS OR EIGHT 4-OUNCE HAMBURGERS

1½ pounds chuck and ½ pound beef shin, ground together
⅓ cup melted butter

PREHEAT THE BROILER

Very gently shape the ground meat into 4 oval steaks or 8 round hamburgers. Whichever shape you choose, they should be almost 1 inch thick. Brush the shaped meat with the melted butter.

For rare, the broiling time should be 5 to 6 minutes on each side. Medium rare takes 6 to 8 minutes. After that, it doesn't really matter.

BEEF STEW IN A PUMPKIN

If there ever was a recipe for Halloween this is it!

SERVES 6

3 tablespoons vegetable oil
2 pounds lean beef chuck, cut into 1-inch cubes
1½ cups coarsely chopped onion
1 small green pepper, coarsely chopped
1 teaspoon finely chopped garlic
4 cups fresh Beef Stock (page 46) or canned chicken broth
1 cup drained canned tomatoes, chopped
½ teaspoon dried oregano
Freshly ground black pepper to taste
1 pound sweet potatoes, peeled and cut into 1-inch cubes
1 pound white potatoes, peeled and cut into 1-inch cubes
1 pound pumpkin meat cut into 1-inch cubes
4 fresh pears, peeled, halved, and cored, cut into ½-inch cubes
2 medium-sized zucchini, washed and cut into ½-inch rounds
One 12-pound pumpkin
Salt to taste

Heat the oil in a 4- or 6-quart casserole, add the meat cubes, and brown on all sides. With a slotted spoon, remove the meat to a bowl and set aside. Add the onion to the casserole and sauté until golden brown. Stir in the garlic and cook a few minutes. Return the meat to the casserole and add the stock, tomatoes, oregano, and pepper to taste. Partially cover the casserole and simmer for 1 hour and 15 minutes. Add the sweet potatoes, white potatoes, pumpkin meat, and pears and cook for 15 minutes. Finally, add the zucchini and cook for an additional 6 minutes. Taste for salt and pepper.

MEATS

PREHEAT THE OVEN TO 350°F

Wash the pumpkin under cold running water. With a small, sharp knife cut down into the top of the pumpkin to create a lid. Pull the stem to release the lid. Scrape all the seeds and the fiber from the lid of the pumpkin and from its cavity.

Place the pumpkin shell and lid on a jelly roll pan and bake on the middle shelf of the oven for 30 minutes.

Remove to a large serving dish, ladle the stew into the pumpkin, and replace its lid.

Serve in individual soup plates.

BEEF AND PORK CHILI

Using cubed meat in place of ground provides texture, and the pork adds a nice flavor.

SERVES 6 TO 8

6 tablespoons lard
1½ pounds beef top round, cut into ½-inch cubes
1½ pounds lean boneless pork, cut into ½-inch cubes
2 cups coarsely chopped onion
1½ teaspoons chopped garlic
6 tablespoons chili powder
1 teaspoon oregano
1 teaspoon ground cumin
1½ teaspoons dried red pepper flakes, crushed
1 small can tomato paste
4 cups fresh Chicken Stock (page 48) or canned broth
Salt to taste
1 cup cooked red kidney beans

In a large, heavy skillet, heat half the lard until it is very hot. Brown the cubed beef and pork in the lard, and as it colors transfer it with a slotted spoon to a 3½- or 4-quart flameproof casserole.

Add the remaining lard to the skillet and cook the onion and garlic until the onion is transparent. Stir in the chili powder, oregano, cumin, red pepper flakes, and tomato paste. Mix with a spoon until all the ingredients are well blended, then gradually add the chicken stock. Pour the mixture over the cubed meat and taste for salt. Bring to a boil and cook, partially covered, for 1 hour, or until the meat is tender. Then add the cooked red kidney beans.

MEAT LOAF WITH JALAPEÑO CHILIES

When ordering more than one kind of ground meat, ask your butcher to wrap them separately. This will ensure that you are getting exactly what you ordered.

SERVES 6 TO 8

2 pounds lean ground beef chuck
1 pound lean ground pork
3 tablespoons butter
1½ cups finely chopped onion
1 tablespoon finely chopped garlic
1 cup Fresh Bread Crumbs (page 12)
1 teaspoon thyme
1 teaspoon salt
3 Jalapeño chilies, seeded and chopped
1 egg
4 slices of bacon

PREHEAT THE OVEN TO 350°F

Put the ground beef and pork in a large bowl. Heat the butter in a medium-sized skillet, add the onion and garlic, and cook until the onion is transparent. Scrape the contents of the skillet on top of the ground meat. Add the bread crumbs, thyme, salt, chilies, and egg. Wet your hands with cold water and knead the mixture until all the ingredients are well blended and smooth.

Shape the meat into a long loaf in a shallow roasting pan and lay the bacon slices on top.

Bake on the middle shelf of the oven for 1½ hours. With a large metal spatula, transfer the meat loaf to a large, heated platter.

*I*RISH *S*TEW

In the Middle East the neck of the lamb is widely used for shish kebab because of its superior flavor. Irish stew probably has never won any culinary awards, but it is a warm, hearty meal, further enhanced by using chicken broth in place of water.

SERVES 6

3 pounds lean, boneless neck of lamb
1 teaspoon salt
Freshly ground black pepper to taste
1/4 cup vegetable oil
3 large onions, peeled and sliced 1/4 inch thick
2 1/2 pounds medium-sized potatoes, peeled
3 cups fresh Chicken Stock (page 48) or canned broth
1 bay leaf
2 tablespoons chopped parsley

Trim the lamb of any fat and cut it into 1½-inch cubes. Toss the cubes of meat with the salt and pepper. In a large, heavy skillet heat the oil until it is very hot. Brown the lamb in the hot fat and remove it to a bowl. Add the onions to the fat and cook until they are transparent, then mix them with the lamb.

Place a layer of potatoes on the bottom of a large, heavy, flameproof casserole, then add a layer of the lamb and onion mixture. Repeat, ending with a layer of potatoes on top. Bring the chicken stock to a boil, add the bay leaf, and pour into the casserole. Return the broth to a boil, reduce to a low simmer, cover the casserole, and cook for about 2½ hours. Check the casserole periodically to make sure the potatoes are not sticking to the bottom. When the meat is tender and most of the liquid has been absorbed by the potatoes, the stew is ready to serve. Sprinkle with the chopped parsley and serve from the casserole.

ℬRAISED 𝒮HOULDER
OF ℒAMB

Lentils go very well with braised lamb. Use the recipe on page 262, Lentils with Cotechino Sausage. Or if you prefer, serve steamed new potatoes with tiny peas. To thicken the braising juices, use 2 teaspoons of arrowroot mixed with a little water or wine. Stir the mixture into the juices in the casserole and cook until the sauce thickens slightly.

SERVES 4

2½ to 3 pounds boned shoulder of lamb
1 teaspoon salt
½ teaspoon freshly ground black pepper
3 tablespoons Clarified Butter (page 283) or vegetable oil
2 cloves garlic
1½ teaspoons dried tarragon
¾ cup dry vermouth

PREHEAT THE OVEN TO 325°F

Season the lamb shoulder with the salt and pepper. Heat the butter or oil in a large, heavy casserole. Brown the meat on all sides. Add the garlic cloves and let them color slightly. Add the tarragon and the vermouth. Cover the casserole and braise the shoulder of lamb on the middle shelf of the oven for 2 to 2½ hours, or until a meat thermometer reaches 150°.

Remove the meat to a hot platter, carve it into thin slices, and strain the juices over it.

127

$\mathcal{B}$OILED $\mathcal{L}$EG OF $\mathcal{L}$AMB
WITH
$\mathcal{C}$APER AND $\mathcal{P}$ARSLEY $\mathcal{S}$AUCE

Although this dish is not common in the United States, it is very popular in Eastern Europe.
Serve the lamb surrounded with winter vegetables.
It is a perfect meal for a cold winter evening.

SERVES 6

LAMB

One 3-to-3½-pound boned leg of lamb, rolled and tied
1 large clove of garlic, cut in half and each half cut into 3 pieces
1 large onion
2 parsnips
1 large carrot
1 rib of celery with leaves, coarsely chopped
1½ teaspoons salt
1 bay leaf

SAUCE

3 tablespoons butter
3 tablespoons all-purpose flour
½ cup capers
½ teaspoon marjoram
¼ cup chopped parsley
2 teaspoons fresh lemon juice
Salt and freshly ground black pepper to taste

128

TO BOIL THE LAMB

Make 6 incisions in the leg of lamb with the tip of a paring knife. Stick a sliver of garlic in each cut. Place the lamb in a large casserole and cover with cold water. Bring to a boil over high heat, skimming off the foam that rises to the surface. Add the onion, parsnips, carrot, celery, salt, and bay leaf. Reduce the heat and simmer, partially covered, for 2½ hours, or until the lamb is tender. Transfer the lamb to a heated platter and cover with foil to keep warm.

TO MAKE THE SAUCE

Measure 2 cups of the lamb stock and strain it through a fine sieve.

Melt the butter in a 1-quart saucepan, stir in the flour, and blend well. Whisk in the 2 cups of lamb stock and cook over high heat until it comes to a boil. Reduce the heat and simmer for 5 minutes, then add the capers, marjoram, parsley, lemon juice, salt, and pepper.

Remove the string from the lamb and slice the meat into ¼-inch-thick pieces. Serve the sauce in a sauce boat.

Broiled Boned Leg of Lamb

Serve the broiled leg of lamb with Tomatoes Provençale (page 232) and Shredded Potato Cakes (page 222). The marinade can also be used for shish kebab.

SERVES 6

½ cup olive oil
¼ cup lemon juice
2 tablespoons prepared mustard
1½ teaspoons oregano
2 bay leaves, crumbled
1 large onion, grated
1½ teaspoons finely chopped garlic
1½ teaspoons coarse salt
1 teaspoon freshly ground black pepper
One 6-to-7-pound boned leg of lamb

In a medium-sized bowl combine the olive oil, lemon juice, mustard, oregano, bay leaves, grated onion, garlic, salt, and pepper. Place the leg of lamb, fat side down, in a large, shallow dish. Beat the marinade with a dinner fork to mix the ingredients thoroughly. Immediately pour the marinade over the boned leg of lamb. Cover with plastic wrap and let the lamb marinate in the refrigerator overnight, turning it a few times.

PREHEAT THE BROILER

Place the lamb, fat side down, on the broiler pan, allowing the marinade ingredients to cling to the meat. Broil the lamb 4 inches from the heat for 15 minutes, then turn it and broil for an additional 15 minutes. Remove the lamb to a large serving platter and allow it to rest for 5 minutes before carving it against the grain into thin slices.

ℛOAST ℒEG OF ℒAMB

Wrapping the slivers of garlic with mint leaves makes a very nice addition to the roast.

SERVES 6 TO 8

One 6-to-7-pound leg of lamb
1 very large garlic clove, cut into slivers
1 tablespoon vegetable or olive oil
2 tablespoons kosher salt
Freshly ground black pepper
½ teaspoon thyme
2 medium-sized onions, peeled
2 small carrots, scraped
2 cups fresh Chicken Stock (page 48) or canned broth

PREHEAT THE OVEN TO 450°F

Make 8 to 10 small incisions on the flat side of the leg. Insert a sliver of garlic in each one. Rub the leg with oil and sprinkle it with the kosher salt, pepper, and thyme. Place the leg, flat side up, in a large, shallow roasting pan. Roast for 30 minutes on the middle shelf of the oven.

Reduce the heat to 350°, add the onions and carrots, and continue to roast for an additional 60 minutes.

Remove the lamb to a heated platter and let it rest for 10 to 12 minutes before carving.

Skim off all the fat from the pan, add the chicken stock, and boil for about 5 minutes. Scrape up all the brown bits in the pan. Strain the liquid through a wire strainer into a small saucepan to keep warm.

Just before serving, pour the warm sauce into a sauce boat.

$\mathscr{B}$ARBECUED $\mathscr{S}$PARERIBS

If you are planning to have dinner outdoors and want to make the cooking as easy as possible, you can start the ribs in the oven early in the day, baking them for the first 30 minutes and finishing them off on the outside grill with the Barbecue Sauce (page 285).

SERVES 4

Salt and freshly ground black pepper to taste
4 pounds spareribs
Barbecue Sauce (page 285)

PREHEAT THE OVEN TO 400°F

Salt and pepper the spareribs on both sides, then place them, rounded side up, on a rack in a large roasting pan. Bake on the middle shelf of the oven for 30 minutes. Brush heavily with the barbecue sauce and continue to bake for 30 to 45 minutes, basting with the sauce about every 10 minutes, or until the ribs are crisp and brown. Cut between the ribs to make individual servings.

*R*OAST *P*ORK
WITH *R*OSEMARY

For family dinners, chop the chine bone in several places and serve with the meat. Bone pickers will love you for it.

SERVES 6

One 5-to-6-pound center-cut pork loin
1 teaspoon coarse salt
Freshly ground black pepper to taste
½ teaspoon rosemary, crushed
¼ cup dry vermouth
1¾ cups fresh Chicken Stock (page 48) or canned broth
2 teaspoons arrowroot mixed with 1 tablespoon water

PREHEAT THE OVEN TO 350°F

Have the butcher remove the chine bone from the loin and tie it back to the loin. Place the pork in a shallow roasting pan. Combine the salt, pepper, and rosemary and rub it on the pork fat. Roast the loin on the middle shelf of the oven for 1½ hours, or until a meat thermometer reaches 170°.

Remove the roast to a warm platter and cover with foil. Skim off all the fat from the pan. Add the dry vermouth and chicken stock, scraping the brown bits that cling to the bottom and sides of the pan. Stir in the dissolved arrowroot and simmer a few seconds or until the sauce has thickened. Remove the string and chine bone and slice the meat into ¼-inch-thick pieces. Serve the sauce in a sauce boat.

$\mathscr{B}$RAISED $\mathscr{S}$AUERKRAUT
WITH $\mathscr{M}$EAT

This recipe is a takeoff from the famous choucroute garni, which reminds me of my first meal in Paris. It was January 1957, and the boat train from Le Havre to Paris lost my luggage, making my arrival at the Pont Royal Hôtel on Rue de Bec quite late. We decided to stroll along the Boulevard St. Germain to find a place to have supper. We came upon the famous Brasserie Lipp, and it was there I had my first choucroute garni.

If you wish, you can make this recipe the day before and reheat it over low heat or in a 300° oven.

SERVES 6 TO 8

1/3 cup lard
2 cups finely chopped onion
1 cup diced carrots
4 pounds sauerkraut
3 sprigs parsley
1 bay leaf   } *tied together into a bouquet garni*
8 juniper berries
1 cup dry white wine
4 cups fresh Chicken Stock (page 48) or canned broth
Salt and freshly ground black pepper to taste
1½ pounds uncooked garlic pork sausage
6 smoked loin pork chops cut ½ inch thick
6 to 8 boiled potatoes

PREHEAT THE OVEN TO 400°F

Heat the lard in a large, heavy casserole with a tight-fitting cover. Add the onion and carrots and cook until the onion is soft but not brown. Stir in the sauerkraut and add the bouquet garni. Pour in the white wine and chicken stock and taste for salt and pepper. Bring the liquid to a boil, cover the casserole, and place on the middle shelf of the preheated oven. Reduce the heat to 325° and braise the sauerkraut for 3 hours.

Prick the sausages in several places and add them to the casserole along with the smoked pork chops. Cook for an additional 30 minutes.

To serve, mound the sauerkraut on a large, deep platter and arrange the meat and boiled potatoes around it. Don't forget to pass the mustard!

$\mathscr{P}$ORK $\mathscr{C}$UTLETS WITH $\mathscr{R}$ED $\mathscr{P}$EPPER

After you allow the sauce to simmer for 15 minutes you can stop, if you wish, for a half hour or so and then proceed with the recipe.

SERVES 4

2 teaspoons finely chopped garlic
½ teaspoon salt
¼ teaspoon freshly ground black pepper
1½ pounds pork cutlets
¼ cup olive oil
1 cup all-purpose flour
2 large sweet red peppers, seeded, deribbed, and cut into ¼-inch strips
½ cup dry white wine
1½ cups fresh Chicken Stock (page 48) or canned broth
2 teaspoons fresh lemon juice
2 teaspoons chopped parsley

In a small bowl combine the garlic, salt, and pepper and with a teaspoon mash the garlic into a paste. Spread the paste on the pork cutlets, wrap them in plastic wrap, and marinate at room temperature for 2 hours.

Heat the oil in a large skillet until it is very hot. Dredge the pork cutlets in the flour, then, two or three at a time, brown them on both sides and transfer them to a plate. Add the red peppers to the skillet and toss them in the remaining fat for 3 to 5 minutes.

Return the pork cutlets to the skillet, pour in the white wine and chicken stock, bring to a boil, reduce the heat, and simmer tightly covered for 15 minutes.

With a slotted spoon, transfer the pork and peppers to a heated platter.

Bring the liquid to a boil, scraping the brown bits from the bottom and sides of the skillet. Continue to cook until the sauce thickens slightly. Stir in the lemon juice and spoon the sauce over the pork and peppers. Sprinkle with the chopped parsley and serve.

$\mathscr{S}$ALTIMBOCCA

After you place the prosciutto on the scallopine, you may stop and proceed with the recipe about 15 minutes before serving.

SERVES 4

1½ pounds veal scallopine
½ teaspoon salt
Freshly ground black pepper to taste
½ cup all-purpose flour
½ cup Clarified Butter (page 283)
½ teaspoon dried sage
6 thin slices prosciutto
8 tablespoons butter (1 stick)
½ cup dry Marsala wine
2 pounds cooked fresh spinach
2 hard-cooked eggs, sliced

Place the veal between two pieces of wax paper and pound it with a mallet into thin slices. Salt and pepper the scallopine and lightly dust with flour. Heat the clarified butter in a large skillet until it is very hot. Cook the scallopine, a few pieces at a time, until golden on both sides.

Remove the veal from the pan and drain the pieces on paper towels.

Sprinkle the veal with the dried sage. Cut the prosciutto slices in half and lay a piece on each scallopine.

Discard the fat from the skillet and wipe it clean. Melt 4 tablespoons of the butter in the skillet. Place all the veal in the pan, add the Marsala wine, and cook for 10 minutes.

Reheat the cooked spinach in the remaining 4 tablespoons of butter.

Cover the bottom of a large, heated platter with the spinach. Arrange the veal on top. Decorate the veal with the sliced egg and pour the juices from the skillet over the scallopine.

ℬRAISED 𝒮MOKED ℋAM

This is a nice change from the ubiquitous baked ham. Served with the Purée of Yellow Split Peas on page 226 and a green vegetable, it is sure to give your dinner parties a new dimension.

SERVES 8 TO 10

One 10-to-12-pound precooked ham
1 *bay leaf*
2 *tablespoons tomato paste*
3 *cups dry red wine*
2 *small onions, peeled and sliced*
2 *whole cloves*
2 *tablespoons softened butter*
2 *tablespoons all-purpose flour*

PREHEAT THE OVEN TO 350°F

With a sharp knife, remove the rind from the ham and reserve. Trim the ham of most of its fat, leaving only a thin layer.

Place the ham on a rack in a shallow roasting pan and bake un-covered on the middle shelf of the oven.

Place the rind in a saucepan and cover with cold water. Add the bay leaf and bring to a boil, reduce the heat to low, and simmer partially covered for 30 minutes.

Strain the liquid into a bowl and discard the rind.

Mix the tomato paste with 2 cups of rind stock. Pour the rind stock and red wine over the ham. Add the onions and cloves to the pan. Braise the ham, basting every 20 minutes or so. In total the ham should braise for about 4 hours.

Remove the ham to a large, heated platter. Skim all the fat from the surface of the liquid in the pan. Mix the softened butter with the flour and stir it into the liquid in the pan. Bring the liquid to a boil, scraping up all the brown bits from the pan. Reduce the heat and simmer the sauce for a few minutes. Strain through a wire sieve into a small saucepan to keep warm. Just before serving, pour into a sauce boat.

$\mathscr{V}$EAL $\mathscr{K}$IDNEYS WITH $\mathscr{A}$RMAGNAC

Because veal kidneys toughen easily, they should be cooked very quickly in very hot butter.

Enjoy the veal kidneys with fried potatoes and the Arugula Salad on page 265.

SERVES 4

4 veal kidneys with all fat removed
Salt and freshly ground black pepper to taste
4 tablespoons Clarified Butter (page 283)
½ cup Armagnac
½ cup heavy cream
2 teaspoons lemon juice
1 tablespoon chopped parsley

Cut the kidneys crosswise ⅓ inch thick. Remove all white tissue. Lightly salt and pepper the slices. In a large, shallow skillet, heat the clarified butter, add the sliced kidneys and cook them, turning once, for 2 minutes. Add the Armagnac and ignite. With a slotted spoon, remove the kidneys to a plate. Add the heavy cream to the skillet and cook until reduced slightly. Taste for salt and pepper, stir in the lemon juice, and return the kidneys to the skillet to reheat them. Do not allow the sauce to boil. Sprinkle with the chopped parsley and serve.

$\mathscr{S}$TUFFED $\mathscr{V}$EAL $\mathscr{C}$HOPS

You can get a head start with the recipe by stuffing the veal chops in the morning.

SERVES 4

1 *pound fresh spinach, cooked and squeezed dry in a towel*
¼ *pound chopped prosciutto*
2 *tablespoons freshly grated Parmesan cheese*
4 *veal chops, about 1½ inches thick*
Salt and freshly ground black pepper to taste
¾ *cup all-purpose flour*
6 *tablespoons Clarified Butter (page 283)*
3 *tablespoons Marsala wine*
¾ *cup fresh Chicken Stock (page 48) or canned broth*
1 *tablespoon softened butter*

Combine the spinach, prosciutto, and Parmesan cheese in a small bowl and set aside.

With a small, sharp knife make an incision through the side of each chop about 3 inches deep. Season the pockets with a little salt and pepper. Using a spoon or your fingers, pack the spinach mixture into the pockets and secure the openings with toothpicks or small metal skewers.

Dredge the chops in the flour and shake off the excess. In a heavy 12-inch skillet heat the clarified butter and sauté the chops in the hot butter for 4 to 5 minutes on each side, or until they are a rich, golden brown. Transfer the chops to a warm platter.

Pour the fat from the skillet, add the Marsala wine and chicken stock, and with a metal spatula scrape all the brown bits from the pan. Remove from the heat and swirl in the softened butter. Pour the sauce over the chops and serve.

$\mathscr{M}$EDALLIONS OF $\mathscr{V}$EAL
WITH $\mathscr{M}$ORELS

In Paris to do research work I dined one evening at the Restaurant Le Laurent on the Avenue Gabriel. I greatly enjoyed this veal dish. It was cooked to perfection, the veal as white as could be with a slightly pinkish center, and buttered egg noodles made the perfect accompaniment.

SERVES 6

3 ounces dried morels
Six 1-inch medallions of veal, cut from a boned loin
Salt and freshly ground black pepper to taste
1 cup plus 4½ teaspoons all-purpose flour
6 tablespoons Clarified Butter (page 283)
3 tablespoons finely chopped shallots
¼ cup cognac
½ cup fresh Chicken Stock (page 48) or canned broth
1¼ cups heavy cream
1 or 2 drops fresh lemon juice

Place the morels in a heatproof dish, cover them with boiling water, and soak for 30 minutes.

SET OVEN ON WARM

Season the medallions with salt and pepper and dredge them in 1 cup of the flour, coating them evenly.

Heat the clarified butter in a large skillet. Shake off any excess flour from the medallions and sauté them in the hot butter for 5 to 6 minutes on each side until they are golden brown. Remove the medallions to a large platter and keep them warm in the oven.

Pour all but 2 tablespoons of the butter from the pan, add the

142

shallots, and cook for a few minutes; add the drained morels. Pour in the cognac, which will ignite spontaneously—BE CAREFUL. Stir in the remaining 4½ teaspoons of flour, then the chicken stock. Bring the sauce to a boil and thicken. Add the heavy cream and simmer for a few minutes, then taste for salt and pepper and add the lemon juice. Spoon the sauce over the veal and serve at once.

𝒱ITELLO 𝒯ONNATO

Served with plain sliced tomato or cold asparagus, Vitello Tonnato makes a wonderful summer luncheon and always becomes the star of a cold buffet.

SERVES 8

VEAL

3½ pounds boneless, very lean veal roast, tied
1 large garlic clove, cut into thin slices
6 cups fresh Chicken Stock (page 48) or canned broth
1 cup white wine
1 cup water
2 medium-sized onions
2 carrots
3 celery stalks
1 bay leaf
8 peppercorns

SAUCE

1 cup olive oil
1 egg yolk
One 7-ounce can tuna fish packed in olive oil
6 anchovies, washed
3 tablespoons lemon juice
½ cup of the strained stock
3 tablespoons capers
½ cup heavy cream
Salt and freshly ground white pepper to taste

TO PREPARE THE VEAL

Make incisions in the veal and insert a sliver of garlic in each one.

Place the veal in a large pot. Add the chicken stock, white wine, water, onions, carrots, celery, bay leaf, and peppercorns. If the liquid does not cover the meat completely, add more wine or chicken stock. Bring the liquid to a boil slowly, reduce the heat, and simmer for 1 hour and 45 minutes, or until the veal is tender. Remove the pot from the heat and let the veal cool in its liquid. Strain ½ cup of the liquid and set aside.

TO MAKE THE SAUCE

Place the olive oil, egg yolk, tuna fish, anchovies, lemon juice, strained stock, and capers in the container of a food processor. Process until the mixture becomes a smooth purée. The sauce should coat a spoon heavily. If the sauce is too thick, add more stock. Refrigerate the sauce in a bowl covered with plastic wrap.

TO ASSEMBLE

When the veal has cooled to room temperature, remove it from the stock, wrap it in plastic wrap, and refrigerate for 2 hours, or until the meat is firm. The stock should be strained and frozen for future use.

Remove the sauce from the refrigerator, beat in the heavy cream, and taste for salt and pepper. Spread one-third of the sauce on the bottom of a large, shallow platter. Remove the veal from the refrigerator and cut away the string. With a sharp knife, slice the veal into ¼-inch slices. Place the slices on the sauced platter and cover with the remaining sauce. Place the Vitello Tonnato in the refrigerator, covered with plastic wrap, overnight.

Remove the Vitello Tonnato from the refrigerator 1½ hours before serving. If you like, you may garnish the veal with chopped hard-cooked egg yolks, chopped parsley, and capers.

$\mathscr{B}$RAISED $\mathscr{V}$EAL WITH
$\mathscr{A}$NCHOVY AND $\mathscr{L}$EMON

This expensive cut of meat calls for a great supporting cast such as Shredded Potato Cakes (page 222) and Boiled Asparagus (page 199).

SERVES 6 TO 8

1 tablespoon grated lemon rind
1 teaspoon finely chopped garlic
1/4 cup flat-leaf parsley, chopped
3 anchovies, washed under cold water, dried, and finely chopped
6 tablespoons softened butter
One 5-pound boned loin of veal
Salt and freshly ground black pepper
1/2 cup finely chopped onion
1/2 cup finely chopped carrots
1/2 cup finely chopped celery
1 cup dry white wine
2 cups fresh veal stock or Chicken Stock (page 48) or canned broth

PREHEAT THE OVEN TO 350°F

In a small bowl, combine the lemon rind, garlic, parsley, anchovies, and 2 tablespoons of the butter. Mix together until well blended. Set aside. Spread the veal loin out flat, cut side up, and season it with freshly ground black pepper and just a little salt. Spread the anchovy mixture on the surface of the meat. Roll the loin jelly-roll fashion and secure it in several places with kitchen twine.

Heat the remaining 4 tablespoons of butter in a large casserole or Dutch oven. Add the onion, carrots, and celery and cook until they just start to brown. Then place the veal on top of the vegetables, add the wine and stock, bring the liquid to a boil, cover the casserole, place it in the lower third of the oven, and braise the veal for about 1½ hours or until tender.

Transfer the veal to a large cutting board and cover loosely with foil for 10 minutes.

In the meantime, place the casserole on high heat and reduce the braising liquid by one-third. Strain it into a small saucepan and keep warm.

Cut away the string from the veal. With a sharp knife, slice the veal thin and arrange the slices on a large, heated platter. Spoon some of the braising liquid on the sliced meat and serve the remainder in a sauce boat.

$\mathscr{T}$RIPE $\mathscr{S}$TEW

This stew takes at least 12 hours to cook, so you should plan on making it the day before. In this case, don't degrease the sauce. The fat will solidify in the refrigerator and you can easily remove it before reheating the stew.

SERVES 6 TO 8

4 pounds ready-to-cook tripe
1 calf's foot, split
3 large onions, coarsely chopped
2 carrots, sliced
3 large leeks, including 2 inches of green, sliced and washed under cold
    running water
2 teaspoons finely chopped garlic
1 teaspoon dried thyme
2 bay leaves
1/2 teaspoon freshly ground black pepper
2 cups dry white wine
4 cups fresh Chicken Stock (page 48) or canned broth
1 cup applejack liqueur
1/4 cup beef suet, chopped
3 sprigs parsley
Salt to taste

Cut the tripe into 1½-inch squares—scissors may work better than a knife. Place the cut tripe in a large pot and set a colander on top. Put the pot in the sink and allow cold water to run into the pot and overflow. When the water runs clear and the tripe is thoroughly cleaned, drain it in the colander.

Place the calf's foot in a pot with water to cover; bring to a boil and boil for 2 to 3 minutes. Drain and set aside.

PREHEAT THE OVEN TO 250°F

Place the tripe and the calf's foot in a large casserole with a tight-fitting cover. Stir in the onions, carrots, leeks, garlic, thyme, bay leaves, pepper, white wine, chicken stock, applejack, beef suet, and parsley sprigs. Bring just to a boil and taste for salt. Cover tightly, place on the middle shelf of the oven, and bake for 12 to 14 hours, or until the tripe is tender. Remove the calf's foot, parsley sprigs, and bay leaf. Using a soup ladle, degrease the sauce. Serve with boiled potatoes sprinkled with chopped parsley.

FISH AND SHELLFISH

ℋOT 𝒮HRIMP 𝒮ALAD

This is just one of many excellent dishes created by Chef Kenneth Pulomena at John Clancy's restaurant in New York City's Greenwich Village. He serves it in soup plates, lined with radicchio.

SERVES 4

1 large leek
24 shrimp (31/35 count), peeled and deveined
Salt and freshly ground black pepper to taste
⅓ cup walnut oil
2 tablespoons sherry wine vinegar
2 tablespoons chopped flat-leaf parsley

Remove the roots and all but 2 inches of the green from the leek. Cut in half lengthwise and wash under cold running water to remove any grit. Slice the leek into long, thin strips and set aside.

Season the shrimp lightly with salt and pepper. Heat the walnut oil in a large skillet, add the shrimp, and cook for 3 to 4 minutes, stirring constantly, until they are slightly firm. Add the sherry wine vinegar, then, with a slotted spoon, transfer the shrimp to individual heated serving plates. Add the sliced leek to the skillet and cook until the leek is wilted, then spoon the contents of the pan over the shrimp. Sprinkle with the parsley and serve.

153

$\mathscr{D}$EEP-$\mathscr{F}$RIED $\mathscr{S}$HRIMP $\mathscr{C}$AKES

In place of shrimp you can use 1 cup of thinly sliced mushrooms or sweet potatoes to make deep-fried vegetable cakes.

SERVES 4 TO 6

¾ cup all-purpose flour
1 cup water
1 egg plus 1 extra yolk
1 teaspoon finely chopped garlic
½ teaspoon ground cilantro
1½ teaspoons salt
⅛ teaspoon cayenne pepper
2 finely chopped scallions
1 carrot, scraped and cut into 1-inch julienne strips
¼ cup finely chopped celery
1 cup cellophane noodles, crushed
12 small shrimp (22/25 to the pound), shelled and deveined
Vegetable oil for deep-fat frying

Combine the flour, water, egg, egg yolk, garlic, cilantro, salt, and cayenne pepper in a large, shallow bowl. With a wire whisk beat the mixture until the ingredients are well blended and smooth. Stir in the scallions, carrot, celery, cellophane noodles, and shrimp.

PREHEAT THE OVEN TO ITS LOWEST TEMPERATURE

Fill one-third of a large cast-iron skillet with the vegetable oil. Using a deep-fat-frying thermometer heat the oil to 375°. Ladle in about 2 tablespoons of the shrimp cake mixture. Cook 3 cakes at a time for about 2 minutes on each side until they are crisp. Transfer them to a jelly roll pan lined with paper towels and keep them warm in the oven until all the shrimp cakes have been fried. Serve them garnished with sprigs of fresh cilantro and lemon wedges.

$\mathscr{S}$HRIMP $\mathscr{D}$E $\mathscr{J}$ONGHE

This is another dish that goes back to Chillingsworth on Cape Cod. It was served as a special, often with lobster meat in place of the shrimp.

If you don't have individual ovenproof serving dishes you may use a large, shallow baking dish. Cover a tray with a napkin and place the baking dish on it. This will make it easy to serve. You may cook the shrimp and make the butter mixture the day before. Just remember to take the butter mixture from the refrigerator several hours before you wish to serve the Shrimp De Jonghe so it will be soft enough to spread on the shrimp.

SERVES 4

¼ pound unsalted butter, softened
1½ teaspoons finely chopped garlic
2 tablespoons finely chopped parsley
1 teaspoon dried tarragon, crumbled
¼ cup grated onion
1 teaspoon salt
Freshly ground black pepper to taste
1 cup dried bread crumbs
½ cup dry sherry
2 pounds cooked medium-sized shrimp, peeled and deveined

PREHEAT THE OVEN TO 450°F

Place the butter in a medium-sized bowl and beat in the garlic, parsley, tarragon, grated onion, salt, pepper, bread crumbs, and sherry.

Divide the shrimp into 4 individual ovenproof serving dishes. Spread the butter mixture on top of the shrimp.

Place the dishes on a jelly roll pan and bake on the top shelf of the preheated oven for 6 to 8 minutes, or until the butter is very hot and the shrimp are heated through.

$\mathcal{S}$HRIMP $\mathcal{R}$ISOTTO

If you don't have much time or just don't want to take the time, this is a perfect dish for the boat, the beach house, or your bridge club.

SERVES 6

8 tablespoons unsalted butter
2 cups long-grain rice
6 cups fresh Chicken Stock (page 48) or canned broth
1 small bay leaf
1 pound small shrimp (22/25 to the pound), shelled, deveined, and
    each shrimp cut into 3 pieces
1 teaspoon finely chopped garlic
Salt and freshly ground black pepper to taste
½ cup grated imported Parmesan cheese
2 tablespoons chopped flat-leaf parsley

Melt 2 tablespoons of the butter in a 2- or 2½-quart heavy casserole. Stir in the rice until the grains glisten. Pour in the chicken stock, add the bay leaf, and bring to a boil. Reduce the heat to low, cover tightly, and steam the rice for 14 to 18 minutes, or until all the stock has been absorbed by the rice. Melt 2 tablespoons of the remaining butter in a medium-sized skillet and add the cut-up shrimp and the garlic. Cook over medium heat just until the shrimp turn pink and are firm to the touch. Season them lightly with salt and pepper. Scrape the contents of the skillet, juices and all, into the rice and, using a large kitchen fork, gently stir in the shrimp, the remaining 4 tablespoons butter, the cheese, and the chopped parsley. Serve from the casserole.

157

𝒮HRIMP 𝓔TOUFFÉE

Each year fresh, shelled, and packaged crayfish are more readily available in fish markets. If you have never eaten crayfish, I suggest buying 1¾ pounds (shelled) to replace the shrimp. You will find Crayfish Etouffée a delightful experience. Also, try serving the Etouffée in pastry shells.

SERVES 4

3 tablespoons butter
1 cup finely chopped onion
1 cup finely chopped scallions
½ cup finely chopped celery
1 teaspoon finely chopped garlic
3 tablespoons all-purpose flour
One 1-pound can plum tomatoes, drained and chopped
2 cups fresh Chicken Stock (page 48) or canned broth
1 tablespoon Worcestershire sauce
2 teaspoons salt
½ teaspoon cayenne pepper
2 pounds small (22/25 to the pound) uncooked shrimp, peeled and deveined

Heat the butter in a 4-quart casserole and add the onion, scallions, and celery. Cook the vegetables until the onion is transparent, then add the garlic and flour, stirring constantly until the flour turns golden brown. Add the chopped tomatoes, chicken stock, Worcestershire sauce, salt, and cayenne pepper, bring the liquid to a boil, reduce the heat, and simmer the sauce, partially covered, for 30 minutes. Taste for seasoning, add the shrimp, and continue to simmer for 3 or 4 minutes, or until the shrimp are firm to the touch.

ℬAKED 𝒮TUFFED 𝒥UMBO 𝒮HRIMP WITH 𝒫ROSCIUTTO

At fish markets jumbo shrimp are referred to as "under 10's," meaning that there are 10 or under to the pound. This recipe can be prepared early in the day and stored in the refrigerator.

SERVES 4

26 jumbo shrimp, peeled and deveined
12 saltine crackers
8 tablespoons unsalted butter, melted, plus 2 tablespoons softened butter
1/4 cup chopped flat-leaf parsley
1/2 teaspoon chopped garlic
2 tablespoons dry sherry
1/4 teaspoon freshly ground black pepper or to taste
12 thin slices of prosciutto
4 lemon wedges

Finely chop 2 of the shrimp and place them in a medium-sized bowl. Crush the crackers into small pieces with your hands and add them to the chopped shrimp along with the melted butter, parsley, garlic, sherry, and pepper. Mix all the ingredients well and set aside.

Butterfly the remaining shrimp by cutting down the back almost all the way through to the underside.

PREHEAT THE OVEN TO 400°F

One at a time, stuff each butterflied shrimp with about 1½ teaspoons of the stuffing mixture. Cut the prosciutto in half crosswise and wrap a piece around each shrimp to hold the stuffing. Secure the prosciutto with a toothpick.

Grease a large, shallow baking dish with the 2 tablespoons of softened butter. Place the shrimp in the dish and bake them on the top shelf of the preheated oven for 10 minutes.

Serve immediately, garnished with the lemon wedges.

𝒞URRIED 𝒮HRIMP

This is a very hot curry. In addition to plain boiled rice, you might like to serve it with papadums, chopped hard-cooked egg, mango chutney, sliced banana, and chopped peanuts. A dollop of yogurt on each portion adds a nice touch.

SERVES 4 TO 6

1½ teaspoons cumin seeds
1½ teaspoons mustard seeds
½ teaspoon dried pepper flakes
½ teaspoon black peppercorns
6 tablespoons butter
¾ cup chopped onion
1½ teaspoons turmeric
2½ teaspoons ground ginger
4 large tomatoes, blanched, peeled, seeded, and coarsely chopped
1½ cups fresh Chicken Stock (page 48) or canned broth
36 medium-sized shrimp
½ cup chopped scallions
Salt

Place the cumin seeds, mustard seeds, dried pepper flakes, and peppercorns in the container of a food processor and process until the spices are pulverized.

Heat the butter in a large, heavy skillet, add the onion, and sauté until transparent. Add the spices from the processor plus the turmeric and ginger. Cook for 3 to 4 minutes over low heat.

Add the chopped tomatoes and turn the heat up to high. Cook the tomatoes until all the water has been cooked off or until the tomatoes reduce to a purée.

Add the chicken stock, then the shrimp and chopped scallions. Simmer the shrimp for 4 to 6 minutes, or until they are firm.

Taste for salt and serve with plain white rice.

160

SHRIMP IN GREEN SAUCE

This is actually a pesto sauce, which works very well with shrimp. If fresh basil is not available you can get some very good commercial pesto sauces. You'll need two 8-ounce containers if you substitute.

SERVES 6

3 cups fresh basil leaves, tightly packed
1 teaspoon salt
Freshly ground black pepper to taste
1½ teaspoons finely chopped garlic
¼ cup pine nuts
¼ cup freshly grated imported Parmesan cheese
1½ cups olive oil
6 tablespoons unsalted butter
2 pounds large shrimp, peeled and deveined

Place the basil leaves in a large wire strainer and wash them under cold running water. Dump them out onto paper towels and pat dry. Strip the leaves from their stems.

Combine the basil, salt, pepper, garlic, pine nuts, Parmesan cheese, and ½ cup of the olive oil in the container of a food processor. Process until the contents are a smooth purée. Every few seconds push the ingredients down with a rubber spatula. Add the remaining olive oil. Continue to process until you have a smooth sauce. Heat the butter in a large skillet until very hot. Add the shrimp and stir them with a large spoon. Cook the shrimp until they turn pink. Add the green sauce and bring to a boil. Serve at once.

ARTICHOKES STUFFED WITH SHRIMP

Believe it or not, the artichokes can be prepared the day before and reheated the next day. After the artichokes have been stuffed and steamed for 20 minutes, allow them to cool to room temperature. Cover with plastic wrap and store them in the refrigerator. Remove the artichokes from the refrigerator 2 hours before serving to let them come to room temperature. Add more water to the casserole, bring the water to a boil, reduce the heat to a simmer, and steam the artichokes, covered, for 15 minutes.

SERVES 6

2 tablespoons salt
6 artichokes, about 4 to 5 inches in diameter at the base
1 lemon, cut in half
½ pound plus 6 tablespoons softened butter
6 cups Fresh Bread Crumbs (page 12)
1½ cups finely chopped onion
2 teaspoons finely chopped garlic
1¼ pounds cooked, peeled and deveined shrimp, finely chopped
2 cups grated imported Parmesan cheese
½ cup flat-leaf parsley, coarsely chopped
2 teaspoons finely chopped fresh lemon peel
½ teaspoon oregano
Salt and freshly ground black pepper to taste

Place 6 quarts of water in a 12-quart pot, add 2 tablespoons salt, and place over high heat. Bring the water to a boil.

In the meantime, trim the bases of the artichokes with a sharp knife until they are flat. Snap off any bruised leaves. With scissors trim off the tips of the rest of the leaves. Rub all the cut leaves with the lemon to prevent discoloring. When the water has come to the boiling point, drop in the artichokes and the remaining lemon. Return the water to a boil and cook the artichokes over high heat for 15 to 20 minutes. Test the artichokes for doneness by piercing the base with the point of a paring knife.

Place a large colander in the sink. With large tongs, remove the artichokes one by one from the water to the colander base up to allow them to drain.

Heat ½ pound of the butter in a large, heavy skillet set over medium heat. Add the bread crumbs and stir until the crumbs are golden. With a large spoon scrape the crumbs into a large bowl and set aside.

Clean the skillet with paper towels and add the remaining 6 table-spoons of butter. When the butter is hot add the onion and garlic and stir. Cook until they are soft but not brown.

Scrape the onion and garlic over the bread crumbs and add the shrimp, grated cheese, parsley, lemon peel, and oregano. With a large spoon toss the ingredients together thoroughly. Taste for salt and pepper. To stuff the artichokes uniformly, divide the stuffing into 6 portions.

Starting with the outer leaves, gently ease them away from the base. With a small spoon push the stuffing down between the outer leaf and the inner leaf, then press the outer leaf back into place. Repeat this process until all the outer leaves have been stuffed. Place the artichoke upright on a large square of aluminum foil and twist the foil ends securely at the top. Stuff and wrap the remaining artichokes the same way. Thirty minutes before serving, stand the artichokes upright in a large flameproof casserole. Fill the casserole with 1 inch of water and cover with foil. Bring the water to a boil, reduce to a simmer, and steam the artichokes for 20 minutes.

$\mathscr{S}$HRIMP, $\mathscr{O}$YSTER, AND $\mathscr{C}$RAB $\mathscr{G}$UMBO

Traditionally a mound of hot boiled rice is placed in the soup plate and the gumbo ladled over it.

I prefer serving it this way, but the choice is up to you. I also feel strongly about the amount of Tabasco sauce that should be added to the gumbo; I believe it should be up to the guests to add their own to taste.

SERVES 6 TO 8

4 tablespoons butter
1 pound fresh okra, washed and thinly sliced
½ cup finely chopped onion
½ cup diced green pepper
1 teaspoon finely chopped garlic
3 tablespoons flour
2 cups canned tomatoes, drained and chopped
5 cups fresh Chicken Stock (page 48) or canned broth
1 bay leaf
½ teaspoon thyme
1 tablespoon Worcestershire sauce
Salt to taste
1 pound small shrimp, peeled and deveined
14 shucked oysters
1 pound lump crabmeat
2 tablespoons chopped flat-leaf parsley

Heat the butter in a large casserole and add the okra, onion, green pepper, and garlic. Cook the mixture, stirring constantly, for 5 minutes, or until the onion is transparent. Stir in the flour and cook for 2 minutes. Then add the tomatoes, chicken stock, bay leaf, thyme, Worcestershire sauce, and salt to taste. Bring the mixture to a boil, reduce the heat, and simmer the

164

mixture, partially covered, for 30 minutes. Add the shrimp and cook for 3 minutes, then add the oysters and cook for 2 minutes. Finally, add the crabmeat and chopped parsley and remove the casserole from the heat.

Serve the gumbo in heated soup bowls with a bottle of Tabasco sauce on the side.

$\mathscr{C}$LAMS IN $\mathscr{B}$LACK $\mathscr{B}$EAN $\mathscr{S}$AUCE

If you wish, just before adding the cornstarch and sherry, drop in a dozen or so small peeled and deveined shrimp. Because the sauce is so rich, I like to serve boiled rice with this dish.

SERVES 4 TO 6

2 tablespoons vegetable oil
1 tablespoon Chinese fermented black beans, finely chopped
1½ teaspoons finely chopped garlic
¼ pound ground pork
½ cup dry white wine
1 tablespoon Japanese soy sauce
¼ teaspoon sugar
Freshly ground black pepper to taste
48 littleneck clams
1 cup fresh Chicken Stock (page 48) or canned broth
3 scallions, including 2 inches of the green tops, finely chopped
1 tablespoon fresh chopped cilantro
3 tablespoons cornstarch dissolved in 3 tablespoons dry sherry
Fresh cilantro for garnish

Heat a large wok or 12-inch skillet with a lid over high heat. Pour in the vegetable oil, add the black beans and garlic, and stir for a few seconds. Add the pork and stir-fry until the meat is no longer pink. Stir in the white wine and cook briskly until almost all of the liquid has cooked away. Stir in the soy sauce, sugar, pepper to taste, and chicken broth.

Place the clams, hinged side down, in the wok or skillet, cover, and cook for 8 to 10 minutes, or until the clams open. (Discard any that don't open.)

With a pair of tongs or a slotted spoon, remove the clams to a warm serving dish. Stir the chopped scallions and cilantro into the broth. Add the cornstarch-sherry mixture to the sauce. Cook, stirring constantly, until it thickens. Pour the black bean sauce over the clams and garnish with large sprigs of cilantro.

DEEP-FRIED IPSWICH CLAMS

There are many deep-fried foods that can be kept warm in a low oven. But I always serve Ipswich Clams immediately and very informally in the kitchen along with a big bowl of Tartar Sauce (page 295).

SERVES 6 TO 8

2 eggs
1½ cups milk
1½ cups flour
Vegetable oil for deep-fat frying
1 quart Ipswich clams, shucked and drained*
Salt and lemon wedges to taste

Beat the eggs in a large bowl and gradually add the milk. Place the flour in a large, shallow plate (a large pie pan works well).

Pour enough vegetable oil into a large cast-iron skillet to come two-thirds of the way up the sides. Heat the oil to 375° using a deep-fat-frying thermometer.

A handful at a time, drop the clams into the milk mixture, then dredge them in the flour. Place the clams in a large wire strainer and shake the excess flour from the clams over the sink.

Carefully drop the clams into the hot oil. Gently separate them with a slotted spoon so they don't cook together but will brown evenly. This will take no longer than 2 minutes. Drain the clams on paper towels. Repeat this procedure until all the clams have been deep-fried. Serve them with salt and lemon wedges.

---

* Not every fish store has Ipswich clams, but most any fish market will be glad to order them for you. They come freshly shucked and packed in tins.

Oysters and Bacon on a Skewer

Because oysters retain excessive amounts of water, use caution when lowering the skewers into the hot oil.

SERVES 6 TO 8

6 slices of bacon, cut crosswise into 8 equal pieces
4 dozen freshly shucked oysters with their liquor
Vegetable oil for deep-fat frying
Freshly ground black pepper to taste
6 to 8 lemon wedges

Place the bacon in a large, heavy skillet and cook it until it turns translucent. Do not allow the bacon to become brown and crisp. Remove from the pan and set aside.

Place the oysters and their liquor in a clean skillet and, over low heat, stirring constantly, cook them until they are *just* plump. Immediately remove them to a plate lined with paper towels to cool.

String the bacon and oysters alternately on bamboo skewers.

PREHEAT THE OVEN TO WARM

Fill a large cast-iron skillet two-thirds full of vegetable oil. Using a deep-fat-frying thermometer, heat the oil to 375°. Gently place the skewers a few at a time into the hot oil, turning them with a slotted spoon and cooking until the bacon is crisp, about 3 minutes. Transfer them to a baking sheet lined with paper towels and keep warm in the oven until all the oyster and bacon skewers are deep-fried. Serve at once, garnished with the lemon wedges.

CHILLED MUSSELS PILAV

This recipe is of Turkish origin, which accounts for the spelling of pilaf. For a first course you will manage well serving 8 to 10 people.

SERVES 6

6 dozen mussels in their shells
4 cups water
¾ cup olive oil
2½ cups finely chopped onion
½ cup pine nuts
2 cups long-grain rice
⅓ cup dried currants
¾ teaspoon ground cinnamon
¼ teaspoon allspice
1 teaspoon salt
¼ cup fresh chopped mint

Scrub the mussels with a brush under cold running water. Pull the beards from the shells and discard. Place the mussels in a large casserole, add the water, and bring to a boil. Cover tightly, reduce the heat, and steam the mussels for about 10 minutes, or until the shells are open. If after 12 minutes there are some that didn't open, discard them. Remove the opened mussels to a colander and allow them to cool. Reserve the cooking liquid.

Heat the olive oil in a 6- or 8-quart casserole, add the chopped onion, and cook until transparent. Stir in the pine nuts and cook for a few minutes. Stir in the rice, currants, cinnamon, and allspice, 4 cups of the reserved cooking liquid, and the salt. Bring to a boil over high heat, reduce the heat to low, cover tightly, and simmer until all the liquid has been absorbed by the rice, about 20 minutes.

Remove the mussels from their shells and stir them into the cooked rice. Let the pilav cool to room temperature, then place it in the refrigerator to chill.

Serve on a platter or on individual plates. Whichever you choose, sprinkle with the chopped fresh mint.

*L*OBSTER À L'*A*MÉRICAINE

This is one of the most popular specials in John Clancy's restaurant. We make the Américaine sauce with canned tomatoes for consistency of flavor. If you plan to make the recipe in August or September, when vine-ripened tomatoes are available, by all means use fresh.

Replace the 3 cups of canned tomatoes with 5 to 6 large fresh tomatoes, blanched, peeled, seeded, and chopped.

SERVES 4

SAUCE

¼ cup olive oil
¼ cup finely chopped carrots
½ cup finely chopped onion
1 teaspoon finely chopped garlic
3 cups canned Italian plum tomatoes with their liquid, roughly broken up
1½ cups fresh Chicken Stock (page 48) or canned broth
1 tablespoon tomato paste
1 bay leaf
1 teaspoon dried thyme
1 teaspoon dried tarragon
1½ teaspoons salt
Freshly ground black pepper to taste

LOBSTER

Four 1½-pound live lobsters
¼ cup olive oil
⅓ cup cognac or brandy
½ cup dry white wine
2 tablespoons chopped parsley
Salt and freshly ground black pepper to taste

172

TO MAKE THE SAUCE

Heat the ¼ cup of olive oil in a 2-quart saucepan. Add the carrots, onion, and garlic. Cook the vegetables until they are lightly colored. Add the plum tomatoes, chicken stock, tomato paste, bay leaf, thyme, tarragon, salt, and pepper. Partially cover the pan and simmer for 40 minutes. Purée the sauce through a food mill into a medium-sized bowl and set aside.

TO KILL THE LOBSTER INSTANTLY

Plunge the tip of a sharp knife just behind the eyes of each lobster. Cut the claws from the body, then sever the tail and cut it into three pieces. Divide the body in half lengthwise. Remove and discard the sac and white intestinal vein. Remove the greenish-brown tomalley (liver) and black eggs if there are any and set aside. Sever each large claw at the joint and crack the shells with the flat side of a cleaver. Each lobster will yield nine pieces.

TO COOK THE LOBSTER

Heat the ¼ cup of olive oil in a very large, shallow skillet. Add the lobster pieces and cook them until the shells turn red. Add the cognac or brandy and ignite it. When the flame dies out, add the dry white wine and reduce it by half. Pour the sauce over the lobster pieces, bring to a boil, and reduce heat to a simmer. Cover the skillet and simmer the lobster for 12 minutes. Beat the tomalley and eggs together until smooth.

Remove the lobster to a large serving platter. Stir the tomalley into the sauce along with the chopped parsley. Cook for 2 to 3 minutes, taste for salt and pepper, and spoon the sauce over the lobster.

$\mathscr{M}$OUSSE OF $\mathscr{S}$EA $\mathscr{S}$CALLOPS

Never use frozen scallops for this recipe. Frozen scallops retain a great deal of water. When the timbales are baking, the mousse mixture will extrude this water, which will cause a considerable amount of shrinkage.

Serve the scallop timbales with Sauce Nantua (page 290) or if you wish, use Hollandaise Sauce (page 293), adding 2 tablespoons chopped dill.

MAKES 12 TIMBALES

10 ounces sea scallops
1 tablespoon egg white
1 teaspoon salt
¼ teaspoon white pepper
⅛ teaspoon ground nutmeg
½ cup heavy cream
½ cup heavy cream, whipped

Purée the scallops in the container of a food processor. Add the egg white, salt, pepper, and nutmeg. Gradually add the heavy cream until the mixture is a fine purée. Remove the purée to a medium-sized bowl and chill in the refrigerator until it is very cold.

PREHEAT THE OVEN TO 375°F

Butter twelve 4-ounce timbales.

Fold the whipped cream into the scallop purée.

Fill the timbales two-thirds full of the mousse mixture. Place the timbales in a large, shallow roasting pan. Fill the roasting pan two-thirds full of hot water.

Bake the scallop timbales, covered with a piece of buttered parchment paper, on the middle shelf of the preheated oven for 10 to 12 minutes, or until they puff slightly.

Invert the timbales onto individual serving dishes and serve with the sauce of your choice.

$\mathscr{C}$IOPPINO

Cioppino is the West Coast's answer to bouillabaisse. It's a fisherman's stew and just reading the ingredients list is enough to make you want to take off for your fish store. Don't forget on your way home to buy a couple of loaves of bread from your favorite Italian bakery.

SERVES 6 TO 8

6 tablespoons olive oil
1 cup chopped onion
1 small green pepper, seeded and chopped
1½ teaspoons finely chopped garlic
2 cups canned tomatoes, drained
2 tablespoons tomato paste
1½ cups dry white wine
1½ cups fresh Chicken Stock (page 48) or canned broth
½ teaspoon salt
Freshly ground black pepper to taste
2 small live lobsters, cut into serving pieces*
2 pounds halibut
2 pounds red snapper
1 pound fresh shrimp, peeled and deveined
18 littleneck clams
18 large mussels, washed and bearded
½ cup flat-leaf parsley

Heat the olive oil in an 8-quart casserole. Add the onion, green pepper, and garlic. Cook the vegetables for about 5 minutes. Do not allow them to brown. Add the tomatoes, tomato paste, wine, chicken stock, salt, and pepper. Bring the mixture to a boil, reduce the heat, and simmer the sauce partially covered for 20 minutes.

* See page 173 for instructions on how to kill and cut up the lobsters.

175

Add the cut-up lobster and cook tightly covered over high heat for about 5 minutes. Add the fish, cover again, and cook 5 minutes longer. Add the shrimp, clams, and mussels and stir the flat-leaf parsley into the sauce. Cover again and boil an additional 5 minutes, or until the clams and mussels open. Discard any that remain closed.

Serve the Cioppino from the casserole with garlic bread.

ℱISHERMAN'S 𝒮TEW

Any of the fish in this recipe can be replaced with other varieties, but because of cooking times they must be of the same size and thickness, and all the fish must be white meat.

SERVES 8

BROTH

½ cup olive oil
2½ cups coarsely chopped onion
6 cups water
2 cups dry white wine
2 pounds fish heads and bones
3 pounds fresh tomatoes, coarsely chopped
½ cup coarsely chopped fresh fennel
2 large garlic cloves, crushed
1 long strip fresh orange peel
1 teaspoon dried thyme
1 large sprig parsley
2 bay leaves
½ teaspoon crushed saffron threads
2 teaspoons salt
½ teaspoon freshly ground black pepper

GARLIC PEPPER SAUCE

1 large green pepper, chopped
2 pimientos
4 large garlic cloves
8 tablespoons olive oil
¼ cup dry bread crumbs
Tabasco sauce to taste

177

SEAFOOD

Four 1½-pound live lobsters, cut up (see Lobster à l'Américaine, page 172)
1½ pounds 1-inch-thick halibut steaks
1½ pounds red snapper, head removed, and cut crosswise into 1-inch-thick steaks
1½ pounds sea bass, head removed, and cut crosswise into 1-inch-thick steaks
2 pounds large mussels, bearded and well scrubbed
2 pounds sea scallops
12 large croutons made from French bread

TO MAKE THE BROTH

Heat the olive oil in a large pot, add the chopped onion, and cook until transparent. Add the water, white wine, fish heads and bones, tomatoes, fennel, garlic, orange peel, thyme, parsley, bay leaves, saffron, salt, and pepper. Bring the liquid to a simmer and cook for 30 minutes. Strain the broth through a fine sieve into another large pot.

TO MAKE THE GARLIC PEPPER SAUCE

Place the green pepper in a small saucepan with water to cover and simmer for about 10 minutes, or until the pepper is tender. Drain and pat dry with paper towels. Place the green pepper, pimientos, garlic, and olive oil in the container of an electric blender. Blend until the mixture turns into a smooth paste. Transfer the mixture to a small bowl. A little at a time, add enough bread crumbs to make the mixture hold its shape on a spoon. Beat in Tabasco sauce to taste and set aside.

TO ASSEMBLE THE STEW

Boil the lobsters in the strained broth for 5 minutes. Add the fish and boil 5 minutes more, then add the mussels and the sea scallops and boil an additional 5 minutes.

Remove the fish to a large, heated platter. Remove the lobster to a second platter. Add a little broth to the garlic pepper sauce. Place a crouton in each soup plate and ladle in the broth. Arrange the fish and shellfish on top.

Serve the garlic pepper sauce from a sauce boat.

$\mathscr{S}$TRIPED $\mathscr{B}$ASS IN $\mathscr{B}$RIOCHE

This dish is wonderful to look at, and serving it with the Hollandaise Sauce on page 293 and a cucumber salad dressed with a little vinegar and oil makes a great brunch menu.

SERVES 6 TO 8

BRIOCHE

2 *envelopes active dry yeast*
A pinch of sugar
1 *cup milk, scalded and allowed to cool to 110 to 115°F*
4 to 4½ cups all-purpose flour
1¾ teaspoons salt
10 egg yolks
¾ cup unsalted butter, softened

FISH

4 to 5 pounds striped bass, cleaned, with head and tail left on
2 tablespoons butter
Salt and freshly ground black pepper to taste
Fresh thyme, basil, and parsley
1 egg beaten with 1 tablespoon milk (for glaze)

TO MAKE THE BRIOCHE

Mix the yeast, sugar, and milk together. Place the flour in a large mixing bowl. Add the salt, egg yolks, and softened butter. When the yeast mixture starts to foam, add it to the flour mixture. Stir all the ingredients with a wooden spoon until the liquid has been absorbed by the flour. Place the dough on a lightly floured work surface. Knead the dough by pushing

179

it forward and folding it in half on top of itself. Repeat the kneading for about 10 minutes, or until the dough is smooth.

Place the dough in a clean bowl that has been lightly buttered. Turn the dough in the bowl so it will be lightly coated with the butter. Let the dough rise until double in bulk (about 1 hour). After the dough has risen, punch it down with your fist to its original size. Cover with plastic wrap and place in the refrigerator until the fish is ready to be assembled.

TO ASSEMBLE THE BRIOCHE

PREHEAT THE OVEN TO 375°F

Wash the bass inside and out and dry with paper towels. Make a pattern of the fish on parchment paper. Divide the dough in half. Roll out half the dough a little wider and longer than the fish. Place the dough on a buttered baking sheet. Place the fish on top and season with salt and pepper. Stuff the cavity with the fresh herbs. Roll out the remaining dough and use the pattern to cut out the shape of the fish. Brush the bottom piece of the dough with the glaze all around the fish. Place the fish-shaped dough on top of the fish, pressing and sealing the edges of both layers of dough. Trim the bottom piece of dough to match the top. Brush the entire surface of the brioche with the remaining glaze. Snip the dough with scissors to make scales and mark the tail lines. Let the dough sit for 15 minutes before baking. Bake on the middle shelf of the preheated oven for 40 to 45 minutes, or until deep golden brown.

$\mathscr{F}$ILLETS OF $\mathscr{S}$TRIPED $\mathscr{B}$ASS EN $\mathscr{P}$APILLOTES

If striped bass is not available, you may substitute red snapper. If parchment paper is not available, you may cook the fish in aluminum foil. Whichever way you do it, always cut the papillote open at the table.

SERVES 4

MUSHROOM TOPPING

2 tablespoons unsalted butter
⅓ cup finely chopped shallots
½ pound finely chopped fresh mushrooms
1 tablespoon flour
2 tablespoons heavy cream
½ teaspoon salt
¼ teaspoon freshly ground black pepper
¼ teaspoon dried thyme
3 tablespoons chopped flat-leaf parsley

FILLING

5 tablespoons softened butter
Four 6-ounce pieces of fillet of striped bass
½ teaspoon salt
4 tablespoons dry vermouth
4 medium-sized mushrooms, thinly sliced

PREHEAT THE OVEN TO 450°F

Heat the butter in a medium-sized skillet, add the shallots, and cook until they are soft but not brown. Add the mushrooms and cook, stirring

181

until the ingredients are well blended. Reduce the heat to low, cover the pan, and cook for 15 minutes. Remove cover, turn the heat to high, and allow the liquid to evaporate. Remove from the heat. Stir in the flour, cream, salt, pepper, thyme, and parsley. Place the pan over low heat and cook until the mixture thickens. Transfer it to a bowl and cool to room temperature.

TO ASSEMBLE THE PAPILLOTES

Cut four sheets of parchment baking paper into 12 x 14-inch heart shapes. Brush each sheet with a teaspoon of the softened butter. Fold each heart lengthwise, then open it and place a fillet alongside the center crease of each heart. Divide the salt evenly among the fillets. Spread the mushroom mixture evenly on top. Dribble 1 tablespoon of dry vermouth on top of the mushroom mixture. Now garnish each portion with one sliced mushroom. Fold the paper over the fillets so the edges meet. Seal the hearts by crimping and rolling the edges at about 1-inch intervals. Before crimping the bottom of the heart, blow through the hole to inflate the papillote.

Place the papillotes side by side on a large cookie sheet. Brush the top of each papillote with the remaining softened butter. Place the cookie sheet on the middle shelf of the preheated oven and bake for 12 minutes. Serve the papillotes on individual plates, and with sharp scissors cut them open at the table.

$\mathscr{F}$RIED $\mathscr{S}$EA $\mathscr{B}$ASS IN AN $\mathscr{O}$RIENTAL-$\mathscr{S}$TYLE $\mathscr{S}$WEET AND $\mathscr{S}$OUR $\mathscr{S}$AUCE

Please, when using a recipe calling for soy sauce, don't use the super-market variety. It's an extremely important ingredient and should be pur-chased in a specialty store.

SERVES 4 TO 6

SEA BASS

Three 1½-pound sea bass, with heads and tails left on
½ **cup all-purpose flour**
½ **cup cornstarch**
½ **cup Japanese soy sauce**

Oil for deep-fat frying

SWEET AND SOUR SAUCE

2 **tablespoons vegetable oil**
1½ **teaspoons finely chopped garlic**
1 **sweet red and 1 sweet green pepper, seeded, deribbed, and cut into long**
  ¼**-inch-wide strips**
1 **carrot, scraped and cut into strips 1 inch long and ¼ inch wide**
1 **cup fresh Chicken Stock (page 48) or canned broth**
6 **tablespoons sugar**
6 **tablespoons red wine vinegar**
1 **tablespoon soy sauce**
2 **tablespoons cornstarch dissolved in 2 tablespoons cold water**

183

TO PREPARE THE SEA BASS

Clean the sea bass under cold running water, pat dry with paper towels, and set aside. Combine the flour, cornstarch, and soy sauce in a small bowl. Using a wooden spoon, mix the ingredients until they form a paste. With your fingers, spread the paste inside and outside the fish and set aside.

TO MAKE THE SWEET AND SOUR SAUCE

Heat the oil in a medium-sized skillet, add the garlic, green and red pepper, and carrot. Cook the vegetables, stirring constantly with a spoon, for 2 to 3 minutes, or until they darken in color a bit. Pour in the chicken stock, sugar, vinegar, and soy sauce. Boil the mixture for 2 minutes. Stir the cornstarch and water mixture and cook for a.few seconds, or until the sauce has thickened, and set aside.

TO FRY THE SEA BASS
PREHEAT THE OVEN TO THE LOWEST TEMPERATURE

Fill a large cast-iron skillet half full with vegetable oil. Using a deep-fat-frying thermometer heat the oil to 350°. Deep-fry two of the sea bass for 12 to 14 minutes, or until they are golden brown. Transfer them to a jelly roll pan lined with paper towels and keep them warm in the oven until the third sea bass has been fried.

One by one, transfer the fish to a platter, setting them on the underbelly and gently pressing them into the platter to keep them from falling on their sides.

Return the sauce to a boil and spoon it over the fish, distributing the vegetables as evenly as possible.

BLOWFISH PROVENÇALE

Blowfish didn't arrive on the commercial scene until the early 1940s and was billed as chicken of the sea. When I was a child, blowfish were so plentiful along the shores of Long Island that I caught them with a crabnet. It was not a popular fish in those days; few people knew of its succulent flavor.

SERVES 4

12 blowfish, 6 to 8 ounces each
1 teaspoon salt
Freshly ground black pepper to taste
1½ cups all-purpose flour
12 tablespoons Clarified Butter (page 283)
1 teaspoon finely chopped garlic
¼ teaspoon thyme
2 tablespoons fresh lemon juice
2 tablespoons dry white wine
2 tablespoons chopped flat-leaf parsley

One at a time, pat the blowfish dry with paper towels and season them with the salt and pepper to taste. Place the flour on a large, flat plate and, one at a time, dredge the blowfish, shaking off any excess flour.

PREHEAT THE OVEN TO THE LOWEST TEMPERATURE

Heat 6 tablespoons of the butter in a large, heavy skillet until hot and sauté half of the fish about 3 to 4 minutes on each side, or until golden brown. With a slotted spatula, remove the fish to an ovenproof dish and place in the warming oven. Discard the butter in the skillet and wipe it clean with paper towels. Add the remaining butter and sauté the remaining fish in the same manner. Discard all but 3 tablespoons of the butter from the skillet. Add the garlic (do not let it brown), thyme, lemon juice, and white wine. Remove from the heat and stir in the parsley. Spoon the sauce over the fish and serve at once.

$\mathscr{S}$MOKED $\mathscr{H}$ADDOCK $\mathscr{Q}$UICHE

The worst thing that can happen to quiche is overbaking, which turns what should be a delicate custard into a dense, unpleasant-tasting dish.

SERVES 6

1 *fully baked Flaky Pastry Crust (page 332)*
6 *ounces smoked haddock*
Approximately 2 cups milk
1 *small onion, thinly sliced*
1/4 *teaspoon freshly ground black pepper*
1/4 *cup diced green pepper*
3 *eggs*
1 *teaspoon Dijon mustard*
1 3/4 *cups heavy cream*
1/2 *teaspoon salt*
1/4 *cup diced pimiento*
2 *tablespoons grated Parmesan cheese*
1 *tablespoon butter cut into small pieces*

PREPARE THE PIE SHELL

Place the smoked haddock in a small saucepan, add enough milk to cover, scatter the onion over the fish and the pepper on top. Bring the milk to a boil over high heat, reduce to a simmer, and cook the haddock partially covered for 10 minutes, or until the fish flakes easily when pulled with a fork. With a slotted spatula, transfer the cooked fish to a plate. Discard the milk and onion. When it is cool enough to handle, flake the fish, making sure there are no bones.

Cook the green pepper in a small saucepan with about 1 1/2 cups of water for about 8 minutes, or until the pepper is tender. Drain the pepper and dry it with paper towels.

PREHEAT THE OVEN TO 400°F

Place the eggs in a large bowl and, with a wire whisk, beat them until they are well mixed, then gradually beat in the Dijon mustard, heavy cream, and salt.

In a small bowl gently toss the cooked fish, cooked green pepper and diced pimientos. Place this mixture on the bottom of the fully baked pie shell.

Pour the egg mixture on top. Sprinkle with the Parmesan cheese and dot with the butter.

Place the quiche on the middle shelf of the preheated oven, reduce the heat to 350°, and bake for 25 to 30 minutes, or until the custard has set.

Serve the quiche hot or warm.

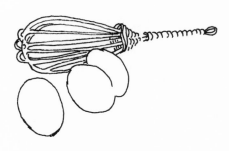

$\mathscr{S}$ALMON $\mathscr{R}$OULADE WITH $\mathscr{H}$OLLANDAISE $\mathscr{S}$AUCE

Actually this is a fallen soufflé. For a great brunch or an elegant first course it will serve 8 to 10.

SERVES 6

2½ teaspoons salt
1 pound fresh salmon
4 tablespoons unsalted butter
¼ cup finely chopped onion
3 tablespoons all-purpose flour
1 cup milk
4 egg yolks
1 tablespoon tomato paste
3 tablespoons chopped fresh dill
1½ teaspoons fresh lemon juice
⅛ teaspoon cayenne pepper
6 egg whites
Hollandaise Sauce (page 293)

Fill a shallow sauté pan half full of cold water and add 1 teaspoon of the salt. Place the salmon in the water and bring to a simmer. Cook the fish 6 to 8 minutes, or until it flakes easily when tested with a fork. Remove the salmon to a plate, and when it is cool enough to handle, remove the skin and bones and then flake the fish.

PREHEAT THE OVEN TO 400°F

Coat a 17½ x 11-inch jelly roll pan with 1 tablespoon of the butter. Line the jelly roll pan with parchment paper and set aside. Melt the remaining 3 tablespoons of butter in a 1-quart saucepan. Add the onion and cook

188

for 3 minutes. Stir in the flour and cook for 2 minutes. Whisk in the milk and slowly bring it to a boil to thicken. Remove from the heat and, one by one, beat in the egg yolks. Add the tomato paste, dill, lemon juice, cayenne pepper, and the remaining 1½ teaspoons of salt. Stir in the flaked salmon and taste the mixture for seasoning.

Beat the egg whites until stiff, then beat one-quarter of the whites into the salmon mixture. Pour the remaining egg white over the salmon mixture and fold them together gently and thoroughly. Scrape the mixture onto the prepared jelly roll pan and, with a rubber spatula, spread the mixture evenly. Place the roulade on the middle shelf of the preheated oven and bake for 15 minutes, or until it has risen and is firm to the touch. While the roulade is baking, make the Hollandaise Sauce.

Remove the roulade from the oven. Pull the parchment paper and the roulade from the jelly roll pan onto the work surface. Spread the Hollandaise Sauce on a large, warm platter. Using the parchment paper as an aid, roll the roulade jelly roll fashion, and with two metal spatulas place it on top of the sauced platter and serve at once.

$\mathscr{S}$HAD WITH $\mathscr{S}$ORREL $\mathscr{S}$AUCE

With the arrival of spring both shad and sorrel appear in the markets. Their flavor combination makes a perfect marriage. Another perfect marriage is the sorrel sauce poured over boiled potatoes. Replace the ½ cup of reduced poaching liquid with Chicken Stock (page 48) and continue with the instructions for the sauce.

SERVES 4

SHAD

4 tablespoons softened butter
2 tablespoons finely chopped shallots
½ teaspoon crumbled dried thyme
1 crumbled bay leaf
4 large mushroom caps, thinly sliced
3 pounds shad fillets
½ teaspoon salt
⅛ teaspoon freshly ground black pepper
1½ cups dry white wine

SORREL SAUCE

Reserved poaching liquid
2 cups heavy cream
1½ tablespoons softened butter mixed with 1½ tablespoons
     all-purpose flour
2 tablespoons butter
½ pound fresh sorrel, washed and shredded
Salt and freshly ground black pepper to taste

TO PREPARE THE SHAD

PREHEAT THE OVEN TO 350°F

Spread 2 tablespoons of the butter over the bottom and sides of a 8 x 12 x 2-inch baking dish. Scatter the shallots, thyme, bay leaf, and half the mushroom caps over the bottom of the dish. Place the fillets, skin side down, in the baking dish.

Sprinkle with the salt and pepper, then dot the fillets with the remaining butter. Scatter the rest of the mushroom caps over the fillets and pour in the wine. Cover the dish with a piece of buttered parchment paper or aluminum foil. Poach the shad on the middle shelf of the preheated oven for 20 minutes.

Transfer the shad to a heated platter and keep warm. Strain the liquid from the baking dish through a fine sieve into a small saucepan.

TO MAKE THE SORREL SAUCE

Bring the poaching liquid to a boil and reduce to ½ cup. Reduce the heat to low and whisk in the heavy cream and the butter-flour mixture (*beurre manié*). Return to a boil and reduce the sauce to 1½ cups. Heat 2 tablespoons of butter in a heavy skillet, stir in the shredded sorrel, and cook for 3 to 4 minutes, or until the sorrel has wilted. Scrape the sorrel into the reduced sauce and taste for salt and pepper. With paper towels, blot up any liquid that might have accumulated on the serving platter. Pour the sorrel sauce over the shad and serve at once.

*E*SCABECHE OF *S*OLE

The fish can be prepared the day before. If you do so, be sure to remove it from the refrigerator several hours before serving time. If you are planning to include this dish for a large buffet, double or triple the recipe to suit your needs.

SERVES 4 TO 6

SOLE

2 pounds fillet of sole, cut into 2-inch pieces
¾ teaspoon salt
1 cup all-purpose flour
12 tablespoons Clarified Butter (page 283)

DRESSING AND GARNISH

2 tablespoons fresh lemon juice
2 tablespoons white wine vinegar
¾ cup olive oil
½ teaspoon dry mustard
½ teaspoon salt
Freshly ground white pepper to taste
1 large lemon, thinly sliced
½ cup tiny Mediterranean black olives
1 tablespoon finely chopped parsley

TO PREPARE THE SOLE

Pat the pieces of sole with paper towels and season with the salt. Place the flour on a large, flat plate and dredge the fish, one piece at a time, shaking off any excess. Heat 6 tablespoons of the butter in a large, heavy skillet until hot. Sauté the fish 2 to 3 minutes on each side, or until they are

192

golden brown. With a slotted spatula, remove the fish to paper towels to drain. Discard the butter in the skillet and wipe the skillet clean with paper towels. Add the remaining butter to the skillet and cook the remaining fish in the same manner. Arrange the fish attractively in a shallow serving dish.

TO MAKE THE DRESSING AND GARNISH

Combine the lemon juice, white wine vinegar, olive oil, dry mustard, salt, and white pepper in a small bowl. Beat the mixture with a fork until the ingredients are well blended. Immediately pour the dressing over the cooked fish.

Garnish the platter with the lemon slices, black olives, and a sprinkling of chopped parsley. Allow the escabeche to rest for about 1 hour at room temperature before serving.

$\mathscr{G}$RILLED $\mathscr{S}$WORDFISH

If you can get fresh tuna fish it can be prepared in the same manner.

SERVES 4

3 tablespoons fresh lemon juice
4 tablespoons Japanese soy sauce
2 tablespoons tomato paste
4 tablespoons sesame oil
1 teaspoon finely chopped garlic
1 teaspoon oregano
½ teaspoon salt
Freshly ground black pepper to taste
Four 8-ounce swordfish steaks, cut about 1 inch thick

Combine the lemon juice, soy sauce, tomato paste, sesame oil, garlic, oregano, salt, and black pepper. Turn the swordfish in the marinade to coat evenly. Baste the steaks every so often, and marinate the swordfish for at least 2 hours at room temperature.

PREHEAT BROILER

Place the steaks on the broiler pan and broil them for 5 minutes on each side, basting with the marinade two or three times until done.

BAKED BROOK TROUT
WITH MUSHROOMS

Frozen trout is probably as prevalent in this country as frozen shrimp. Frozen shrimp is very acceptable, but frozen trout is not. Try to find a fish market that uses a trout tank so you will be sure to get fresh trout. There is a big difference in flavor.

SERVES 4

Four 10-to-12-ounce fresh brook trout, heads and tails left on
1 teaspoon salt
Freshly ground black pepper to taste
8 tablespoons Clarified Butter (page 283)
½ pound fresh mushrooms
1 tablespoon fresh lemon juice
1 cup chopped scallions
¼ cup dry vermouth
2 tablespoons chopped parsley

PREHEAT THE OVEN TO 450°F

Wash the trout under cold running water and pat dry with paper towels. Season the cavities of the trout with the salt and pepper. Heat the butter in a heavy skillet, add the mushrooms, lemon juice, and scallions and cook for 2 minutes, stirring constantly. Place the trout on top of the mushroom mixture and bake on the middle shelf of the preheated oven for 10 minutes. Using a large metal spatula, transfer the trout to a warm serving plate. Place the skillet (be careful of the hot handle) over high heat and add the dry vermouth and the chopped parsley. Cook for 2 minutes and pour over the trout.

VEGETABLES

$\mathscr{B}$OILED $\mathscr{A}$SPARAGUS

While the asparagus spears are still hot, toss them with melted butter, pepper, and salt, or serve with Hollandaise Sauce (page 293). For a change, I sprinkle on Fresh Bread Crumbs (page 12) and Parmesan cheese, dot with butter, and broil just to brown the crumbs.

SERVES 4

2 pounds fresh asparagus
3 tablespoons salt

Lay the asparagus spears on your work table and trim their bases until all the stems are the same length. Holding each spear just below the tip, scrape it with a sharp paring knife to remove the tough outer skin. Wash the asparagus under cold running water. Set aside.

Place a large, shallow roasting pan over two burners and add the salt and enough water to come two-thirds of the way up the sides of the pan. Bring the salt water to a boil. Add the asparagus, with all the spears facing in the same direction, and boil them (depending upon the thickness) for 6 to 10 minutes. To test for doneness, pierce the base with the tip of a paring knife; there should be a slight resistance. Using metal tongs, transfer the asparagus spears to a kitchen towel to drain the excess liquid, then to a heated serving platter. If serving the asparagus cold, place the roasting pan in the sink, cover with a kitchen towel, and run cold tap water into the pan until the asparagus is completely cooled. Transfer to a dry kitchen towel to absorb the excess liquid before storing in the refrigerator.

199

ASPARAGUS FRITTATA

For lunch or brunch this frittata goes well with grilled sausages.

SERVES 4

6 eggs
½ teaspoon salt
⅛ teaspoon cayenne pepper
3 tablespoons cold water
2 tablespoons butter
1 cup cooked asparagus (about ¼ pound fresh), cut into ½-inch lengths
6 tablespoons freshly grated imported Parmesan cheese

PREHEAT THE BROILER

Beat the eggs with the salt, cayenne, and cold water. Heat the butter in a 10-inch omelet pan. Add the asparagus and toss in the butter, season with a little salt and pepper, pour in the beaten egg mixture, and cook over medium heat for 2 to 3 minutes, or until the eggs just start to set. Sprinkle the cheese on top of the frittata. Set the pan under the broiler until the eggs puff up slightly. Slide the frittata onto a heated serving dish.

BROCCOLI ROMAN STYLE

This would make a good addition to a hot antipasto, or serve it at room temperature.

SERVES 4 TO 6

2 pounds fresh broccoli
¼ cup olive oil
½ teaspoon finely chopped garlic
¾ cup dry white wine
¾ cup fresh Chicken Stock (page 48) or canned broth
Salt and freshly ground black pepper to taste

With a sharp knife, cut away the thick stems of the broccoli and re-move the green leaves. Gently separate the broccoli into florets and place them in a bowl of cold water.

In a heavy enameled or stainless 12-inch saucepan heat the olive oil until it is very hot. Immediately add the garlic and broccoli florets and toss them with a slotted spoon until they are well coated with the oil. Add the white wine and chicken stock, then cover the saucepan and cook for 15 minutes or until the broccoli is tender. With the slotted spoon, transfer the florets to a heated platter.

Cook the liquid in the saucepan over high heat until it has reduced to half.

Taste for salt and pepper and pour the sauce over the broccoli.

Green Cabbage in White Wine

I particularly enjoy this cabbage with broiled or roasted chicken. When making this recipe, plan to serve it immediately. Reheating the cabbage takes away from its crispness and fresh flavor.

SERVES 4 TO 6

3 to 3½ pounds green cabbage
8 tablespoons unsalted butter
1¼ cups dry white wine
1 teaspoon salt
¼ teaspoon sugar
Freshly ground black pepper to taste

Remove and discard any bruised leaves, then wash the head of cabbage under cold running water. Core the cabbage and cut it in half. Place the flat sides down on a cutting board. Slice the cabbage in ½-inch pieces.

In a heavy enameled or stainless steel 12-inch skillet, heat the butter until very hot. Add the cabbage and toss with a metal spatula until it is well coated with butter. Add the wine, salt, sugar, and pepper to taste.

Bring the wine to a boil, cover, and reduce the heat. Simmer the cabbage for 10 minutes, or until just tender.

Remove the cabbage to a heated platter. Bring the liquid to a boil over high heat, reduce it to half, and pour it over the cabbage.

DEEP-FRIED CAULIFLOWER

During the early 1960s, when I was working with the development and research department of the Green Giant Company, I was taken by some of the staff somewhere in the Valley of the Green Giant for before-dinner drinks. It was in this establishment that I first tasted deep-fried cauliflower. Needless to say, there wasn't much room for dinner!

SERVES 4 TO 6

2 pounds cauliflower
Vegetable oil for deep-fat frying
1 teaspoon salt
¼ teaspoon white pepper
2 beaten eggs mixed with ½ cup milk
1 cup all-purpose flour
1½ cups Fresh Bread Crumbs (page 12)

PREHEAT THE OVEN TO LOWEST TEMPERATURE

With a sharp knife, cut away the base of the cauliflower and remove any green leaves. Gently separate the cauliflower into florets. Cook the florets in salted boiling water for 8 minutes. Drain on paper towels.

Fill a large cast-iron skillet two-thirds full of vegetable oil. Using a deep-fat-frying thermometer, heat the oil to 360°F.

Season the florets with the salt and white pepper. Dip them in the egg-milk mixture, then in the flour. Roll them in the fresh bread crumbs until they are completely covered.

Deep-fry the florets in several batches until they are golden brown.

Transfer them to a jelly roll pan lined with paper towels and keep them warm in the oven until all the cauliflower has been fried.

Transfer the florets to a warm platter and sprinkle with additional salt and pepper before serving.

203

CELERY ROOT AND POTATOES

This flavor combination works well with almost any roast or game.

SERVES 4 TO 6

3 tablespoons butter
4 large shallots, chopped
1 teaspoon chopped garlic
1 pound celery root, peeled and diced
Fresh Chicken Stock (page 48) or canned broth, to cover
1 pound potatoes, peeled and diced
2 teaspoons arrowroot
2 tablespoons cold water
1/4 cup chopped parsley
Salt and freshly ground black pepper to taste

Heat the butter in a 2-quart saucepan and cook the shallots and garlic for a minute or so. Do not allow them to brown. Drop in the celery root and add enough chicken stock to cover. Bring the liquid to a boil, reduce the heat, and simmer for 20 minutes. Add the diced potatoes and additional broth to cover. Continue to cook for 8 to 10 minutes, or until the potatoes are tender. Mix the arrowroot with the cold water and stir it into the liquid. Simmer for 2 to 3 minutes, then mix in the chopped parsley. Taste for salt and pepper and serve immediately.

CORN AND GREEN CHILE SOUFFLÉ

For a stronger cheese flavor sprinkle ¼ cup additional Parmesan cheese over the egg whites when folding them into the sauce. This recipe will serve 4 as a light main course.

SERVES 6

5 tablespoons butter
¼ cup finely chopped onion
5 tablespoons all-purpose flour
1 teaspoon salt
¼ teaspoon white pepper
1 cup milk
5 egg yolks
1½ cups corn kernels, canned or frozen, drained or defrosted
One 4-ounce can green chilies, drained, seeded, and chopped
6 egg whites
2 tablespoons freshly grated imported Parmesan cheese

**PREHEAT THE OVEN TO 400°F WITH
A COOKIE SHEET ON THE MIDDLE SHELF**

Butter the bottom and sides of a 2-quart soufflé dish with 1 tablespoon of the butter and set aside. Melt the remaining 4 tablespoons of butter in a small, heavy saucepan. Add the onion and sauté until transparent. Gradually add the flour, stirring with a wooden spoon until the mixture is smooth, and cook for 4 to 5 minutes. Slowly beat the milk into the flour mixture with a wire whisk. Return the saucepan to the heat and bring to a boil to thicken. Lower the heat and simmer the sauce for a few seconds. Remove from the heat and whisk the egg yolks into the sauce, one at a time. Stir in the corn and chopped green chilies and set aside.

With a large balloon whisk or an electric mixer, beat the egg whites until they form stiff but moist peaks. Stir one-quarter of the egg whites into the sauce, then scrape the sauce over the remaining egg whites. With a large rubber spatula, fold all the ingredients together gently but thoroughly. Carefully pour the mixture into the prepared dish and sprinkle with the cheese.

Place the soufflé on top of the cookie sheet in the preheated oven and bake for 5 minutes. Reduce the heat to 375° and continue to bake the soufflé for 20 to 25 minutes longer, or until it puffs up 2 to 3 inches above the edges of the dish.

CUCUMBERS AU GRATIN

This dish can be served with chops, steaks, or any simple roast. To turn it into a light luncheon dish, increase the sauce recipe by half and add 1 cup of partially cooked shrimp. In this case the recipe will serve 4. You might also like to sprinkle additional Parmesan cheese on top of the bread crumbs.

SERVES 6

CUCUMBERS

3 large, firm cucumbers
2 tablespoons butter
¼ teaspoon salt
A pinch of cayenne pepper

SAUCE AND TOPPING

4 tablespoons butter
2 tablespoons all-purpose flour
1½ cups milk
¼ teaspoon salt
A pinch of grated nutmeg
1 egg yolk
¼ cup freshly grated imported Parmesan cheese
½ cup Fresh Bread Crumbs (page 12)

TO PREPARE THE CUCUMBERS

Scrape the peel from the cucumbers and slice them in half lengthwise. With a small spoon, scrape out the seeds and discard them. Cut the cucumbers in half crosswise.

Melt the butter in a medium-sized skillet. Add the cucumbers, salt, and pepper and cover the pan. Cook the cucumbers over low heat, shaking the pan occasionally, for 6 to 8 minutes, or until the cucumbers are almost tender. With a slotted spoon, remove the cucumbers to a shallow baking dish and set aside.

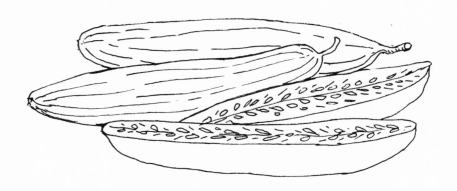

TO PREPARE THE SAUCE AND TOPPING

PREHEAT THE OVEN TO 400°F

Melt 2 tablespoons of the butter in a small, heavy saucepan, add the flour, and cook for 2 minutes, then whisk in the milk. Bring the sauce to a boil to thicken, reduce the heat, and cook for 3 minutes. Remove from the heat and beat in the salt, nutmeg, egg yolk, and cheese. Taste for seasoning. Discard any water that may have accumulated in the baking dish. Pour the sauce over the cucumbers, sprinkle with the bread crumbs, and dot with the remaining butter.

Bake the cucumbers on the middle shelf of the oven for 12 to 14 minutes, or until the sauce is bubbly and the crumbs are toasty brown.

CREAMED ENDIVE WITH HAM

Since this dish requires reheating, it can be made hours in advance. It is perfect for brunch or informal suppers. Small steamed new potatoes go well with the endive and ham.

SERVES 6 TO 8

8 to 10 large, firm endive
8 tablespoons unsalted butter
¾ teaspoon salt
Freshly ground white pepper to taste
¼ cup fresh lemon juice
¼ cup all-purpose flour
1 cup fresh Chicken Stock (page 48) or canned broth
1 cup heavy cream
A pinch of grated nutmeg and white pepper
8 to 10 very thin slices boiled ham
½ cup freshly grated imported Gruyère cheese

PREHEAT THE OVEN TO 325°F

Clean the endive with dampened paper towels, discarding any bruised leaves. Trim the stems and with the point of a vegetable peeler, hollow the stems.

Butter a large, shallow baking dish with 2 tablespoons of the butter. Place the endive in the baking dish and sprinkle with ½ teaspoon of the salt, pepper, and lemon juice. Dot the endive with 2 additional tablespoons of butter. Cover the dish and bake on the middle shelf of the preheated oven for 1 hour, or until tender. Remove from the oven and let cool.

Melt the remaining 4 tablespoons of the butter in a small saucepan. Add the flour and cook for 2 minutes. Whisk in the chicken stock and heavy cream and bring the mixture to a boil to thicken. Reduce the heat to low and cook for 5 minutes. Add the remaining ¼ teaspoon of salt, the nutmeg, and white pepper and remove the sauce from the heat.

RESET THE OVEN TEMPERATURE TO 400°F

When the endive is cool enough to handle, wrap each stem in a slice of ham and return to the baking dish.

Pour the sauce over the endive and sprinkle with the grated cheese. Bake the endive for 20 to 25 minutes, or until bubbly hot.

$\mathscr{S}$HREDDED $\mathscr{K}$ALE

This is one of those vegetables that isn't much good until it feels the first frost. It goes very well with the Braised Smoked Ham on page 138.

SERVES 6 TO 8

4 pounds kale
½ cup lard
1 teaspoon salt
2 tablespoons red wine vinegar

Thoroughly wash the kale under cold running water. Trim away any bruised spots. Cut the leaves from their stems. Gather the leaves by the handful, roll them lengthwise into a cylinder, and shred crosswise. Drop the shredded kale into a large pot of boiling water and cook uncovered for 5 minutes. Drain the kale in a large colander.

Melt the lard in a heavy, large skillet or shallow casserole. Add the kale and sprinkle with salt. Cook, stirring frequently, for 20 to 25 minutes, or until tender. Stir in the red wine vinegar and serve at once.

$\mathscr{S}$TUFFED $\mathscr{K}$OHLRABI

Most people think paprika is a very common spice that can be bought in any supermarket, but it should be bought loose from a food specialty store. If you buy more than you need, store it in a plastic bag in the freezer. This recipe is substantial enough to serve as a main course.

SERVES 4 TO 6

KOHLRABI MIXTURE

8   medium-sized kohlrabi with leaves
3   tablespoons butter
½   cup finely chopped onion
1   teaspoon chopped garlic
1   pound ground lean pork
½   cup dry bread crumbs
2   tablespoons chopped parsley
2   tablespoons sweet imported Hungarian paprika
¼   teaspoon marjoram
2   eggs, lightly beaten
1½   teaspoons salt
⅛   teaspoon cayenne pepper
4   cups fresh Chicken Stock (page 48) or canned broth

SAUCE

2   tablespoons butter
2   tablespoons all-purpose flour
1   cup heavy cream
1   tablespoon sweet imported Hungarian paprika

TO MAKE THE KOHLRABI MIXTURE

Wash the kohlrabi, remove the leaves, and reserve half of them. Slice a thin piece off the top of each kohlrabi and hollow them out (a melon baller works well), leaving a ¼-inch shell. Set the pulp aside. Blanch the reserved leaves in boiling water for 4 minutes. Drain, then chop them, and add to the pulp.

Heat the butter in a large, heavy skillet until it is very hot. Add the onion and cook until lightly browned, add the garlic and cook for 2 minutes longer.

Combine the cooked onion and garlic with the ground pork, bread crumbs, parsley, paprika, marjoram, eggs, salt, and cayenne pepper. Mix well with a wooden spoon.

Stuff the kohlrabi shells with the meat mixture, mounding it above the tops of the shells. Place the stuffed kohlrabi shells in a heavy casserole with a tight-fitting cover. Scatter the pulp, leaves, and any meat mixture that might be left over around them. Add the chicken stock and bring to a boil over high heat. Cover, reduce the heat to low, and simmer for 45 minutes, or until you can pierce the kohlrabi easily with the tip of a paring knife.

TO MAKE THE SAUCE

Melt the butter in a small, heavy saucepan. Add the flour and cook for 2 minutes, then whisk in the cream and paprika. Bring the sauce to a boil to thicken, reduce the heat, and cook for 3 minutes. Remove the kohlrabi to a heated platter. Whisk the sauce into the ingredients in the casserole and return to a boil. Taste for seasoning, then spoon the sauce over the kohlrabis and serve.

WILTED BOSTON LETTUCE

If you would like a slightly sweet-and-sour flavor, add ½ teaspoon of sugar along with the vinegar. A sprinkle of chives is also a nice addition to this dish. Wilted Boston Lettuce goes very well with broiled chicken.

SERVES 6

3 heads Boston lettuce
6 slices bacon
3 tablespoons sherry wine vinegar
Freshly ground black pepper to taste
12 red radishes, thinly sliced

Remove any outer bruised leaves from the lettuce and tear the heads into small pieces. Wash the lettuce thoroughly and set aside in a colander.

Slice the bacon crosswise into ¼-inch-wide pieces. Place the bacon in a heavy skillet, not cast iron or aluminum, and render until crisp. Remove the bits of bacon to a plate and set aside. Add the sherry wine vinegar to the bacon fat and add pepper to taste. Add the lettuce and radishes and stir the greens around in the skillet for 1 to 2 minutes, or until they have wilted. Serve on a heated platter garnished with the crumbled bacon.

$\mathscr{B}$ROILED $\mathscr{M}$ USHROOM $\mathscr{C}$ APS

Quick, simple broiled mushrooms go well with steaks and chops, or serve them on fried toast as a first course.

SERVES 4

16 fresh mushroom caps about 1½ inches in diameter
8 tablespoons butter, melted
Salt and freshly ground black pepper to taste
4 lemon wedges
2 tablespoons chopped flat-leaf parsley

PREHEAT THE BROILER

Wipe the mushroom caps with a damp cloth and place them in a shallow flame-proof baking dish. Dribble the melted butter over them and season with salt and pepper. Toss them around to coat them with the butter. Arrange them hollow side up and broil, turning once, for a total of 5 minutes. Arrange the caps on a serving plate with the lemon wedges. Pour the juices from the baking dish over the mushrooms and sprinkle them with the chopped parsley.

$\mathscr{W}$HITE $\mathscr{T}$URNIPS AND $\mathscr{M}$USHROOMS

The turnips can be cooked hours in advance and finished just minutes before serving time.

SERVES 4 TO 6

1½ *pounds small white turnips*
1 *teaspoon salt*
6 *tablespoons unsalted butter*
1 *pound large fresh mushrooms wiped clean with dampened paper towels
    and quartered*
Salt and freshly ground black pepper to taste
2 *tablespoons chopped parsley*

Peel and wash the turnips. In a 2-quart saucepan, combine them with enough water to cover and add the salt. Bring the water to a boil, reduce to a simmer, and cook the turnips for 15 to 20 minutes, or until tender. Drain in a colander and set aside.

Heat the butter in a 10- or 12-inch skillet over medium heat, add the mushrooms, and cook them for 4 minutes, stirring constantly. Stir in the cooked turnips and season with salt and pepper. When the turnips are hot, serve them in a warm bowl, sprinkled with the chopped parsley.

ROASTED PEPPERS

Wrapping the roasted peppers in a damp cloth creates steam, which enables you to remove the skin quite easily, but for some spots you will have to scrape with a paring knife.

SERVES 6

6 large red or green bell peppers
¾ cup olive oil
¾ cup sherry wine vinegar
¾ cup cold water
1 tablespoon imported sweet Hungarian paprika
1 tablespoon salt
Freshly ground black pepper to taste

PREHEAT THE BROILER

Wash the peppers under cold running water and dry them with paper towels. Place the peppers on the broiler pan and broil them about 4 inches from the heat, turning them until the skins blacken and blister all around.

Remove the peppers from the broiler and wrap them in very damp towels. Set them aside for 10 minutes. In the meantime, combine the olive oil, vinegar, cold water, paprika, salt, and pepper in a medium-sized mixing bowl. Set aside.

Using the damp towels, rub the skins from the peppers. With a wire whisk, beat the oil and vinegar mixture. Add the skinned peppers, turning them about until they are well coated. Cover the bowl with plastic wrap and refrigerate overnight. Remove from the refrigerator at least 1 hour before serving.

These roasted peppers make a wonderful appetizer served with small cubes of feta cheese and scallions.

$\mathscr{P}$OTATO $\mathscr{D}$UMPLINGS

You can also transfer the dumplings to a shallow baking dish, sprinkle with Fresh Bread Crumbs (page 12) in addition to the cheese, and place under the broiler to toast the crumbs a bit.

SERVES 6 TO 8

4 medium-sized boiling potatoes
4 teaspoons salt
¼ teaspoon white pepper
A pinch of nutmeg
2 egg yolks
Approximately 1 cup flour
6 tablespoons butter, melted
6 tablespoons freshly grated Parmesan cheese

Place the potatoes in a large pot and cover with water. Bring to a boil and cook the potatoes for 20 minutes, or until tender. Drain the potatoes in a colander, and when they are cool enough to handle, peel them. Put the potatoes through a ricer into a large bowl. Add the egg yolks and season with 1 teaspoon of the salt, the white pepper, and nutmeg.

Beat in the egg yolks and transfer the riced potato mixture to a lightly floured work surface. Knead in enough flour so that the mixture no longer sticks to your hands. Divide the dough in half and roll each piece into a rope 1 inch in diameter. Break off small pieces of dough and roll them between the palms of your hands, shaping the dumplings into balls 2 inches in diameter.

Bring a large pot of water seasoned with the remaining 3 teaspoons of salt to a boil. Drop in the dumplings and cook them 6 to 8 minutes, or until they rise to the top. With a slotted spoon, transfer them to a large serving platter. Dribble the melted butter over the dumplings and sprinkle with the Parmesan cheese.

German Potato Dumplings

My mother always served these dumplings with sauerbraten. They also go well with Boiled Leg of Lamb with Caper and Parsley Sauce (page 128) or Braised Stuffed Quail (page 110). Use any leftover dumplings the next day, by slicing them into 1/3-inch-thick rounds and frying them in a little butter.

MAKES ABOUT 18 DUMPLINGS

5 medium-sized potatoes
2 eggs
4½ teaspoons salt
⅛ teaspoon nutmeg
¼ teaspoon freshly ground white pepper
¾ cup flour ⎫
¾ cup farina ⎭ mixed together

Place the potatoes in a large pot and cover with water. Bring the water to a boil and cook the potatoes for 20 minutes, or until tender. Drain the potatoes in a colander, and when they are cool enough to handle, peel them. Put the potatoes through a ricer into a large bowl. Beat in the eggs, 1½ teaspoons of the salt, the nutmeg, and white pepper. Gradually beat in the flour-farina mixture until the dough holds its shape lightly.

With lightly floured hands, use ⅓ cup of the dough to shape dumplings slightly larger than golf balls.

Bring a large pot of water seasoned with the remaining salt to a boil. Drop in the dumplings and simmer over medium heat for about 12 minutes, or until they rise to the top. With a large slotted spoon, transfer the dumplings to a warmed platter.

FRENCH-FRIED POTATOES

No one in the world enjoys French-Fried Potatoes as much as the Belgians do. On a recent research trip I was told that after the potatoes are blanched (first frying) they should be refrigerated overnight. This really isn't necessary. What does matter is that they are fried in rendered beef kidney suet. They never achieve a golden brown color, but their flavor is unsurpassed.

After you have fried the potatoes and the fat is cool, strain it and store it in the refrigerator. The fat can be used several times for other treats. Try making home fries or hashed brown potatoes with the leftover beef fat.

SERVES 4 TO 6

6 *pounds ground beef suet*
8 *large baking potatoes*

PREHEAT THE OVEN TO 250°F

Place the ground suet in a large, heavy casserole. Place the casserole on the middle shelf of the oven. As the suet melts and at least 1 inch of liquid appears on the bottom of the casserole, increase the oven heat to 325°.

When the suet is completely liquid, cool it to room temperature and then strain it through two layers of dampened double cheesecloth into a deep-fat fryer or a large cast-iron skillet. The fat should be 3 to 4 inches deep.

Peel the potatoes and slice them lengthwise 3/8 inch thick, then cut the slices 3/8 inch wide. Because of the shape of the potatoes, they will vary in length.

Heat the fat to 330° using a deep-fat-frying thermometer. A handful at a time, plunge the potatoes into the hot fat. Turn them about in the fat so they will cook evenly.

Cook the potatoes for 6 to 8 minutes, or until they become limp. With a slotted spoon, remove the potatoes to a jelly roll pan or large platter. Increase the temperature of the fat to 375°. In the same manner as before, plunge the potatoes into the fat and cook them for 3 to 4 minutes, or until they are lightly brown and crisp.

Drain the potatoes on a jelly roll pan lined with a double thickness of paper towels. Serve at once.

$\mathscr{S}$HREDDED $\mathscr{P}$OTATO $\mathscr{C}$AKES

In Switzerland these potato cakes are called rosti. They are crisp on the out-side and soft in the center. They can be served with chicken, steak, chops, and roasts.

SERVES 4 TO 6

6 large baking potatoes
½ teaspoon salt
Freshly ground black pepper to taste
6 tablespoons Clarified Butter (page 283)

Drop the potatoes into a large pot of boiling water and cook for 12 minutes. Drain the potatoes and when they are cool enough to handle, peel them. Refrigerate the potatoes for about an hour, or until they are cold.

Grate the potatoes into a large bowl, using the large blade of a four-sided grater. Gently toss the shredded potatoes with the salt and pepper.

Heat 3 tablespoons of the butter in a heavy 10- or 10½-inch skillet *with sloping sides* until it just begins to smoke. Drop in all the potatoes and spread evenly with a metal spatula. Shake the skillet once or twice and fry the potatoes for 8 minutes. Use the metal spatula to check the color as they brown.

When the potatoes are a deep golden brown, cover the skillet and invert the potato cake. Add the remaining 3 tablespoons of butter to the skillet and slide the potato cake back into the pan to brown the other side. Continue to fry the potatoes in the same manner. Slide the potato cake onto a warm platter and serve at once.

$\mathscr{P}$OTATOES $\mathscr{P}$ARISIENNE

Store the potato scraps in the refrigerator. The next day you can use them to make mashed potatoes or drain and chop them into small pieces for frying.

SERVES 4

6 large boiling potatoes
4 tablespoons Clarified Butter (page 283)
Salt and freshly ground black pepper to taste

PREHEAT THE OVEN TO 400°F

Peel the potatoes and keep them in cold water. With a melon baller, cut the potatoes into balls. Return the potato scraps to the water for another use.

Heat the butter in a large skillet with an ovenproof handle until it is very hot. Add the potatoes, shaking the pan from time to time so that they brown evenly. Then place them on the middle shelf of the oven and bake for 12 to 14 minutes, or until they are cooked. Test them with the point of a paring knife. Salt and pepper to taste and serve immediately.

$\mathscr{S}$TUFFED $\mathscr{P}$OTATOES
$\mathscr{F}$ISH $\mathscr{H}$OUSE $\mathscr{S}$TYLE

These potatoes can be made the day before for small or large informal gatherings and reheated just before serving. Accompanied by a large tossed green salad with the dressing of your choice, this will be substantial enough to serve as a main course.

SERVES 6

6 *very large baking potatoes*
½ *cup unsalted butter melted in ½ cup heavy cream*
1 *teaspoon salt*
¼ *teaspoon white pepper*
4 *tablespoons grated onion*
2 *tablespoons chopped chives*
2 *tablespoons finely chopped flat-leaf parsley*
1½ *cups freshly grated sharp cheddar cheese*
8 *ounces fresh crabmeat, picked over and cartilage removed*
6 *medium-sized cooked shrimp, peeled, deveined, and cut into ⅓-inch pieces*
2 *tablespoons butter*

PREHEAT THE OVEN TO 400°F

Thoroughly scrub the potatoes under running water. Pat them dry with paper towels and place on the middle shelf of the preheated oven. Bake for 1 hour, or until you can pierce them easily with the tip of a paring knife.

Remove the potatoes from the oven, and when they are cool enough to handle, slice off the tops lengthwise. Scoop out the tops into a bowl and discard the skins. Scrape out the bottoms into the bowl and set the skins aside.

Mash the potatoes, then gradually add the hot butter-cream mixture and continue to mash the potatoes until they are free of lumps. Season the potato mixture with the salt and pepper. Stir in the onion, chives, parsley, cheese, crabmeat, and shrimp. Pack the mixture into the potato skins, mounding it high. Dot the tops of the potatoes with the butter.

Place the potatoes on a jelly roll pan and reheat them on the middle shelf of the oven for 15 to 20 minutes, or until they are heated through.

$\mathcal{P}$URÉE OF $\mathcal{Y}$ELLOW $\mathcal{S}$PLIT $\mathcal{P}$EAS

You will enjoy this purée with grilled pork chops, knockwurst, or the Braised Smoked Ham on page 138.

SERVES 4 TO 6

2 cups yellow split peas
¼ pound salt pork
¾ cup finely chopped carrot
¾ cup finely chopped celery
2 cups finely chopped onion
¼ teaspoon marjoram
6 cups fresh Chicken Stock (page 48) or canned broth
2 tablespoons melted butter
1 large onion, peeled and thinly sliced

Wash and stone the split peas under cold running water. Combine the split peas, salt pork, carrot, celery, onion, and marjoram in a heavy 4- or 5-quart saucepan. Pour in the chicken stock, bring to a boil, reduce the heat to simmer, and cook, partially covered, for about 45 minutes, or until the peas are soft. Remove the salt pork and set aside.

PREHEAT THE OVEN TO 350°F

Purée the peas and vegetables in the container of a food processor. Transfer the purée to a large, shallow baking dish.

Dice the salt pork. Heat the butter in a small skillet and render the salt pork in the butter until it is crisp. Remove the salt pork with a slotted spoon and sprinkle it on top of the split pea purée.

Fry the sliced onion in the fat remaining in the skillet until it is golden brown. Remove the onion and distribute it evenly on top of the casserole.

Bake the purée on the middle shelf of the preheated oven for 20 to 30 minutes. Serve from the casserole.

$\mathscr{S}$TRING $\mathscr{B}$EANS IN $\mathscr{S}$OUR $\mathscr{C}$REAM $\mathscr{S}$AUCE

This is one of the few vegetable dishes you can prepare in advance and reheat without any loss of flavor. One-half teaspoon of marjoram can be a nice addition if you like.

SERVES 6 TO 8

4 quarts water plus 2 tablespoons salt
2 pounds string beans, washed and trimmed
6 tablespoons butter
1 large onion, sliced
1 teaspoon finely chopped garlic
2 tablespoons imported sweet Hungarian paprika
¼ cup all-purpose flour
1½ cups fresh Chicken Stock (page 48) or canned broth
1 cup sour cream beaten with 2 teaspoons flour
Salt and freshly ground black pepper to taste

In a large soup pot, bring the water to a rolling boil with the salt. Drop in the string beans a handful at a time. Return the water to a boil and cook the string beans 10 to 15 minutes, or until they are just tender. Drain the beans in a colander.

Melt the butter in a 10- or 12-inch skillet. Add the onion and garlic and cook over medium heat until the onion is soft. Stir in the paprika, then the flour. Continue to cook a few minutes longer. Add the chicken stock, increase the heat, and bring the stock to a boil. Reduce the heat and let the stock simmer for 2 to 3 minutes. Add the string beans and sour cream and continue to simmer until the beans are heated through and the sauce is hot. Taste for salt and pepper.

Beating the flour into the sour cream keeps it from curdling.

MASHED SUMMER SQUASH

You must make sure that the squash is well drained. If there is still excess water when you start to mash the squash, drain it again. If you like, add a little nutmeg to the recipe.

SERVES 4

2 pounds crook-necked summer squash
2 teaspoons salt
4 tablespoons softened butter, at room temperature
One 3-ounce package of cream cheese, at room temperature
½ teaspoon sugar
Freshly ground black pepper to taste

Scrub the squash under cold running water. Remove the ends and cut the squash crosswise into 1-inch pieces. Put the squash in a large pot and cover with cold water. Add 1 teaspoon of the salt. Bring the water to a boil, reduce to a simmer, and cook the squash, partially covered, for 15 to 20 minutes. The squash should be a little soft.

Drain the squash in a colander. Shake it dry and return it to the pot. Mash the squash with a potato masher. Add the remaining 1 teaspoon of salt, the butter, cream cheese, sugar, and pepper to taste. Continue to mash the squash until the mixture is well blended. Serve immediately.

$\mathscr{S}$UMMER $\mathscr{S}$UCCOTASH

This recipe can be made very successfully with frozen vegetables. Let them defrost completely before proceeding with the instructions.

SERVES 4 TO 6

4 tablespoons butter
2½ cups cooked fresh corn
2½ cups cooked fresh green beans, cut into 1-inch pieces
½ teaspoon sugar
¼ teaspoon imported sweet Hungarian paprika
½ teaspoon salt
1 cup heavy cream

Melt the butter in a shallow 2-quart casserole. Add the corn, green beans, sugar, paprika, and salt. Cook over medium heat for 3 minutes, stirring occasionally. Add the heavy cream, raise the heat to high, and cook the succotash until the cream has reduced by half. Serve immediately.

$\mathscr{P}$ENNSYLVANIA $\mathscr{D}$UTCH $\mathscr{F}$RIED $\mathscr{T}$OMATOES

The first time I ate these tomatoes, I couldn't believe the combination—it is wonderful.

SERVES 4 TO 6

4 medium-sized tomatoes
1½ teaspoons salt
½ teaspoon freshly ground black pepper
6 tablespoons unsalted butter
1 cup all-purpose flour
¼ cup light brown sugar
½ cup heavy cream

Wash and dry the tomatoes and slice both ends off each one. Slice each tomato into 3 pieces horizontally. You should have 12 slices about ¾ inch thick, depending upon the size of the tomatoes.

Season the tomato slices with the salt and pepper. Heat the butter in a heavy 12-inch skillet (not cast iron). Dredge both sides of the tomatoes in the flour and cook them in the butter for 4 to 5 minutes, or until they start to brown on the bottom. With a wooden spoon force half of the brown sugar through a sieve onto the tomatoes. Turn the tomatoes, sprinkle with the remaining brown sugar, and cook 3 to 4 minutes longer. Add the cream and when the liquid starts to boil, remove the tomatoes to a serving dish and turn off the heat. With a wire whisk, blend the contents of the pan and pour over the tomatoes. Serve at once.

Tomatoes Provençale

These easy-to-make tomatoes are an attractive addition to any plate of broiled meat or poultry.

SERVES 4

4 firm, ripe tomatoes 3½ to 4 inches in diameter
1 cup Fresh Bread Crumbs (page 12)
½ cup coarsely chopped flat-leaf parsley
1 teaspoon dried basil
½ teaspoon finely chopped garlic
2 anchovies, washed under cold running water, patted dry, and chopped
2 tablespoons chopped fresh mint
½ teaspoon salt
Freshly ground black pepper to taste
Approximately 4 tablespoons olive oil

Cut the tomatoes in half horizontally and scoop out the seeds with a teaspoon. Sprinkle the tomatoes lightly with salt and turn them upside down on a plate or paper towels to drain.

PREHEAT THE OVEN TO 350°F

Combine the bread crumbs, parsley, basil, garlic, anchovies, mint, salt, pepper, and olive oil in a medium-sized mixing bowl. Mix the ingredients thoroughly. Stuff the cavities of the tomato halves with the crumb mixture, mounding it up in the center. Place the tomatoes in a shallow baking dish and bake on the middle shelf of the oven for about 20 minutes, or until the tomatoes are just tender. The baking time will vary depending upon the firmness of the tomatoes. Serve hot or at room temperature, which I prefer.

𝒮TUFFED 𝒵UCCHINI

*Owning a zucchini corer makes this recipe much easier to execute.
A zucchini corer is a half-round blade about 6 to 8 inches long attached to
a wooden handle. If you can't find one, ask your housewares dealer to order
one.*

This is substantial enough to serve as a main course.

SERVES 6

2 tablespoons olive oil
1 cup finely chopped onion
1 teaspoon finely chopped garlic
2½ cups canned tomatoes, drained and coarsely chopped
2½ cups water
1½ teaspoons salt
8 medium-sized zucchini
1 pound lean ground lamb
1 egg
¾ cup cooked rice
½ teaspoon ground allspice
1 tablespoon chopped fresh mint

Heat the oil in a large, heavy skillet (not cast iron), add the onion
and garlic, and cook until transparent. Add the tomatoes, water, and ½ teaspoon of the salt and bring to a boil over high heat. Reduce the heat to low
and simmer for 45 minutes, partially covered.

Scrub the zucchini under cold running water. Dry them with paper
towels and cut 1 inch off each end. With a long, narrow knife or a zucchini
corer, hollow out the center of each zucchini. Soak the zucchini in cold,
salted water for 10 minutes. Rinse them off under cold running water and
pat them dry with paper towels.

Combine the lamb, egg, rice, the remaining teaspoon of salt, the
allspice, and mint and mix well with a large wooden spoon. Beat ½ cup of

233

the sauce into the ground meat mixture. Put half the meat stuffing at a time into a large pastry bag fitted with a large plain tube, and stuff the zucchini by forcing the mixture through the pastry bag (or use a long-handled spoon). Lower the zucchini into the sauce. Return to a boil, reduce the heat, and simmer the stuffed zucchini for about 30 minutes, or until tender.

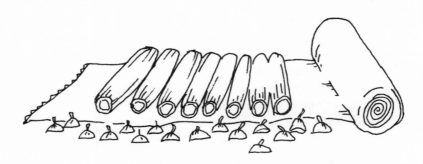

ℤUCCHINI ℙIE

Once in a while, for a pleasant change, I use ¼ cup of imported grated Parmesan cheese in place of the feta cheese.

SERVES 6 TO 8

2¼ cups butter
1 cup finely chopped onion
2 pounds zucchini, coarsely grated
¼ cup chopped flat-leaf parsley
½ teaspoon salt
Freshly ground black pepper to taste
½ cup milk
½ pound feta cheese, crumbled
4 eggs, lightly beaten
14 sheets of filo pastry

Heat ¼ cup of the butter in a 10- or 12-inch skillet. When the butter is hot, add the onion and cook until transparent. Stir in the zucchini and cook, covered, for 5 minutes. Remove the cover and cook the mixture over high heat until the liquid has evaporated. Transfer the zucchini mixture to a large bowl and cool to room temperature. Stir in the parsley, salt, pepper, milk, feta cheese, and beaten eggs.

PREHEAT THE OVEN TO 350°F

Melt the remaining butter. With a pastry brush, grease the inside of a 9- or 10-inch pie plate. One at a time, layer 12 sheets of the filo dough in the pie plate, brushing each sheet with the melted butter. Alternate the direction of the layers so there will be an even amount of pastry around the outer rim of the pie plate. Scrape the zucchini on top of the filo and, with a spatula, spread the mixture evenly.

Fold the ends of the filo over the center of the pie and gently but firmly press them on the filling. Brush the top of the pie with butter. Then layer the last 2 sheets of filo on top of the pie, brushing both sheets with butter. With scissors cut off the excess filo from around the edges of the pie plate. With the tip of a small, sharp knife score 8 portions through the filo.

Bake on the middle shelf of the oven for about 40 minutes, or until the pastry is a deep golden brown.

𝒱EGETABLE 𝒪MELET 𝒮PANISH 𝒮TYLE

With the Tomato Salad on page 274, this omelet makes a wonderful lunch or brunch.

SERVES 4 TO 6

6 tablespoons olive or vegetable oil
¼ cup diced green pepper
¼ cup diced red pepper
1 small onion, thinly sliced
½ cup diced smoked ham
2 baking potatoes, thinly sliced
1 teaspoon salt
Freshly ground black pepper to taste
4 eggs

Heat the oil in a 12-inch cast-iron skillet until very hot. Add the green and red peppers, onion, ham, and potatoes. Cook the vegetables over low heat, turning them from time to time, until the onions are lightly colored. Cover the skillet and cook over low heat for 10 minutes, or until the potatoes are tender. Remove the cover and season the vegetables with ½ teaspoon of the salt and the pepper.

Beat the eggs in a small bowl with the remaining salt. Pour the eggs over the vegetables and continue to cook the omelet until the eggs are firmly set.

Invert the omelet onto a large serving dish, or simply serve it from the pan. Whichever way you choose, this omelet should be cut into wedges.

$\mathscr{S}$TUFFED $\mathscr{V}$EGETABLES $\mathscr{S}$PANISH $\mathscr{S}$TYLE

I enjoy these vegetables served at room temperature, and you might like to try them that way. You will need a good bread for soaking up the juices. This is substantial enough to serve as a main course.

SERVES 4

SAUCE

⅓ cup olive oil
¾ cup chopped onion
1 large clove garlic, finely chopped
¼ cup chopped green or red pepper
4 teaspoons flour
½ cup canned tomatoes, drained and chopped
1¼ cups water
¾ cup dry white wine
2 teaspoons salt

STUFFING

1½ pounds ground lean veal
¼ pound Serrano ham, cut into small dice
1 large onion, coarsely chopped
¼ cup chopped parsley

VEGETABLES

4 firm tomatoes, about 2½ inches in diameter
4 medium-sized bell peppers
2 large zucchini
4 medium-sized boiling potatoes

TO MAKE THE SAUCE

Heat the olive oil in a large skillet and add the onion, garlic, and pepper. Cook over medium heat until the vegetables are soft. Stir in the flour, then add the tomatoes, water, white wine, and salt. Simmer for 15 minutes, then purée the sauce in a food processor and set aside.

TO MAKE THE STUFFING

Process all stuffing ingredients in a food processor until well blended and set aside.

TO PREPARE THE VEGETABLES

Wash the tomatoes, cut a thin slice off the top of each, and with a small spoon (a grapefruit spoon works well) hollow out the tomatoes.

Wash the bell peppers and cut a thin slice off the top of each, remove the seeds, and carefully remove the ribs.

Scrub the zucchini under cold running water. Remove the ends and cut the zucchini in 2-inch lengths. Using a melon baller, make a large cavity in each zucchini round.

Peel and wash the potatoes, cut a thin slice off the top of each, and hollow them out with a grapefruit spoon or melon baller.

TO ASSEMBLE THE STUFFED VEGETABLES

PREHEAT THE OVEN TO 375°F

Stuff the vegetables with the veal mixture. Place the stuffed vegetables, except the tomatoes, in a large, shallow casserole with a tight-fitting cover. Pour the sauce over the vegetables and bake on the middle shelf of the preheated oven for 45 minutes. Add the tomatoes and continue to bake for an additional 20 minutes. Serve hot from the casserole or at room temperature.

Pastas, Grains, and Beans

$\mathscr{K}$REPLACH

Although geographically miles apart, kreplach, wonton, and ravioli are all the same—stuffed noodle dough. And after eating all three most of my life, I still can't make up my mind which is my favorite. Each is very special at the right time and place.

Kreplach may be cooked the day before serving and stored in the refrigerator. Although they are virtually synonymous with chicken soup, try them in the Beef Broth with Marrow and Chives on page 59, or the Escarole Soup on page 63, omitting the cheese. Before serving, let the Kreplach come to room temperature and place a few in each soup plate, then pour the broth or soup over them.

MAKES APPROXIMATELY 48

DOUGH

2 *cups all-purpose flour*
½ *teaspoon salt*
4 *eggs*
3 to 4 *tablespoons cold water*

FILLING

4 tablespoons vegetable oil
1 cup finely chopped onion
¾ pound very lean ground beef
1 egg
1 teaspoon salt
¼ teaspoon freshly ground black pepper
2 tablespoons chopped parsley

TO MAKE THE DOUGH

Place the flour in a medium-sized mixing bowl and add the salt, eggs, and 3 tablespoons water. With a wooden spoon, stir all the ingredients together until the liquid has been absorbed by the flour. With your hands, gather the dough into a ball. If the dough crumbles, add the additional 1 tablespoon of water. Place the ball of dough on a clean, lightly floured surface and knead it for 10 minutes, or until it is smooth and elastic. Set the dough aside, cover with a lightly dampened towel, and allow it to rest for 30 minutes.

TO MAKE THE FILLING

Heat the vegetable oil in a large skillet, add the onion, and cook for about 5 minutes, or until the onion is soft. Stir in the ground beef and break up any lumps so the texture is consistent. Cook the meat until there is no trace of pink. Scrape the mixture into a bowl. Beat in the egg and season with the salt, pepper, and parsley. Set aside to cool.

TO ASSEMBLE THE KREPLACH

On a lightly floured surface, roll out the dough to a square ⅛-inch-thick. It will be about 14 inches. If the dough contracts as you roll it, cover it again with the damp towel for 5 to 10 minutes and then continue to roll until the dough is a perfect square. Place the towel over the dough and allow it to rest for 10 minutes before cutting it into 2-inch squares.

Place 1 teaspoon of the meat mixture in the center of each square. With a small pastry brush or your fingers, brush the edges of the dough with cold water. Fold the dough in half to form a triangle, pressing the edges together firmly.

Bring 3 to 4 quarts of water to a boil with 1 tablespoon of salt and drop in the Kreplach 3 or 4 at a time. Return the water to a boil, reduce to a simmer, and cook uncovered for 12 to 14 minutes. They will rise to the surface as they are done. Taste one to be sure.

Drain in a colander and return the Kreplach to the pot. Run cold water into the pot to stop the Kreplach from cooking and sticking together. Drain again, place on a jelly roll pan, and cover with plastic wrap until ready to serve.

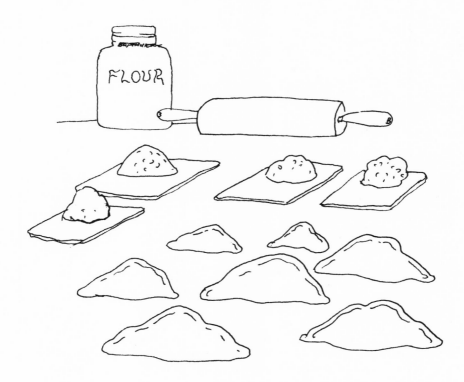

ℬAKED ℒASAGNA

Baked Lasagna is the answer for serving a large crowd of people easily. You can double or triple the recipe, depending upon your needs. Assemble the lasagna the day before and store it in the refrigerator covered with plastic wrap. A note of warning: Drain the lasagna noodles on paper towels that are pure white and free of any decorative colors. I learned the hard way by ending up with blue pears and cherries on my noodles!

SERVES 6 TO 8

MEAT SAUCE

4 tablespoons olive or vegetable oil
¾ pound ground lean veal
¾ pound ground lean beef round
¼ pound ground lean pork
1 cup finely chopped onion
1 teaspoon finely chopped garlic
1 cup white wine
6 ounces tomato paste
3 pounds canned tomatoes and their liquid
1 cup water
1½ teaspoons oregano
2 teaspoons dried basil
1½ teaspoons salt
Freshly ground black pepper to taste

BÉCHAMEL

3 cups light cream
1 teaspoon salt
¼ teaspoon white pepper
⅛ teaspoon nutmeg
4 tablespoons butter
6 tablespoons flour

PASTA

1 tablespoon salt
2 tablespoons olive oil
½ pound fresh lasagna noodles
¾ cup freshly grated Parmesan cheese

TO MAKE THE MEAT SAUCE

In a large, heavy skillet, heat the oil until it is very hot. Stir in the ground veal, beef, and pork. Cook for about 8 minutes, stirring constantly, or until there is no longer any trace of pink.

Stir in the onion and garlic and cook until the onion is translucent. Add the white wine and reduce until all the liquid has cooked away. Add the tomato paste and the tomatoes, water, oregano, basil, salt, and pepper. Bring the sauce to a boil over high heat. Partially cover the pan and turn the heat to simmer. Continue to cook the sauce for 1½ hours.

TO MAKE THE BÉCHAMEL

Place the light cream in a small saucepan and add the salt, pepper, and nutmeg. Heat the cream until it is very hot. Set aside.

Melt the butter in a heavy 1-quart saucepan, add the flour, and stir until smooth. Whisk in the hot cream and place the saucepan over high heat, bringing the sauce to a boil and whisking constantly. When the sauce is very thick, lower the heat and cook for an additional 3 minutes. Remove the sauce from the heat and set aside.

TO MAKE THE PASTA

In a large pot, bring 6 quarts of water to a boil with 1 tablespoon of salt and 2 tablespoons of olive oil. Gradually add the lasagna noodles and stir with a large fork for a few minutes. Boil the noodles over high heat until just tender. Depending upon the thickness of the pasta, the cooking time could be from 6 to 10 minutes. The pasta should be slightly resilient to the bite. Place the pot in the sink and cool the pasta with cold running water. Gently lift out the strips of pasta and drain them on paper towels.

TO ASSEMBLE THE LASAGNA
PREHEAT THE OVEN TO 350°F

Spread a thin layer of the meat sauce on the bottom of a 9 x 12 x 3-inch casserole. Spread about one-third of the béchamel on top. Overlap one-third of the pasta on top of the sauces. Repeat the layering twice more. Top with the remaining meat sauce and béchamel. Sprinkle the Parmesan cheese on top.

Bake in the preheated oven until the lasagna is bubbling hot, about 30 minutes. Remove from the oven and allow the lasagna to rest for 5 minutes before serving.

LINGUINI WITH WHITE CLAM SAUCE

If you prefer, you can make the basic sauce hours before, stopping at the point of returning it to a boil. Continue with the sauce about 15 minutes before serving it.

SERVES 6 TO 8

½ cup olive oil
2 large cloves garlic, peeled and bruised
¼ cup finely chopped onion
½ teaspoon dried red pepper flakes
¼ teaspoon oregano
¼ cup dry white wine
¾ cup fresh clam juice
8 quarts water
1 tablespoon salt
1½ pounds linguini
4 dozen littleneck or topneck clams, shucked

Heat the olive oil in a small saucepan, add the garlic cloves and, gently shaking the pan, cook until the garlic is lightly browned. Add the onion, red pepper flakes, and oregano. Cook the mixture until the onion is transparent. Add the white wine and reduce it by half, then add the clam juice. Return the sauce to a boil and set aside.

Bring 8 quarts of water to a boil with the salt in a large pot. Drop in the linguini one-third at a time, stir with a wooden spoon once or twice, and boil for 8 to 10 minutes, or until just tender. Strain the linguini in a large colander, shaking the colander several times to be sure the pasta is thoroughly drained. Transfer the pasta to a large, heated platter. Bring the sauce to a boil, add the clams, and cook for 1½ minutes. Pour the sauce over the pasta and toss together to serve.

249

$\mathscr{L}$INGUINI WITH $\mathscr{B}$LACK $\mathscr{B}$EAN AND $\mathscr{C}$LAM $\mathscr{S}$AUCE

It's too bad that when Marco Polo's cargo containing noodles bound for Italy was put aboard ship in China, fermented black beans were not included. This dish could have been enjoyed long ago.

SERVES 6 TO 8

2 *tablespoons vegetable oil*
1 *tablespoon Chinese fermented black beans, finely chopped*
½ *teaspoon finely chopped garlic*
¼ *pound ground pork*
1 *tablespoon Japanese soy sauce*
½ *teaspoon sugar*
Freshly ground black pepper to taste
1½ *cups clam broth*
3 *scallions, including 2 inches of the green top, finely chopped*
1 *tablespoon chopped fresh cilantro*
3 *tablespoons cornstarch dissolved in 3 tablespoons of dry sherry*
8 *quarts water*
1 *tablespoon salt*
1½ *pounds linguini*
48 *littleneck or topneck clams, shucked*

Heat a large wok or 12-inch skillet over high heat. Pour in the vegetable oil, add the black beans and garlic, and stir-fry for a few seconds. Add the ground pork and stir-fry until the meat is no longer pink. Stir in the soy sauce, sugar, pepper, clam broth, scallions, and cilantro. Stir in the cornstarch and sherry mixture. Cook, stirring constantly, until the sauce thickens, and set aside.

In a large pot, bring the 8 quarts of water to a boil with the salt. Drop in the linguini, one-third at a time, stir with a wooden spoon once or twice, and boil rapidly for 8 to 10 minutes, or until just tender. Strain the linguini in a large colander, shaking the colander several times to be sure the pasta is thoroughly drained. Transfer the pasta to a large, heated bowl. Bring the sauce to a boil, add the shucked clams, and cook for 1½ minutes. Pour the sauce over the pasta, toss together, and serve.

$\mathscr{S}$PAGHETTI WITH $\mathscr{C}$HICKEN $\mathscr{L}$IVERS

In some circles this recipe is known as Spaghetti à la Caruso, an excellent product of the American melting pot kitchen.

SERVES 6

8 tablespoons olive oil
1½ cups finely chopped onion
1 teaspoon finely chopped garlic
Two 2-pound cans tomatoes and their liquid
3 tablespoons tomato paste
½ teaspoon dried basil
1 bay leaf
2 tablespoons salt
½ teaspoon sugar
1½ pounds chicken livers
Freshly ground black pepper to taste
1 cup flour
1½ pounds spaghetti

Heat 4 tablespoons of the olive oil in a large, heavy skillet. Add the onion and garlic and cook until the onion is transparent, about 8 minutes. Stir in the tomatoes and their liquid, then add the tomato paste, basil, bay leaf, 2 teaspoons of the salt, and the sugar. Bring the liquid to a boil, reduce the heat, and simmer the sauce, partially covered, for 35 to 40 minutes.

Trim the chicken livers of any fat and cut them in half. Sprinkle the livers with 1 teaspoon of the salt and pepper to taste. Dredge them in the flour.

Heat the remaining 4 tablespoons of olive oil in a large, heavy skillet. Add the livers and cook until they are golden brown. Remove them from the skillet and set aside.

252

Bring a large pot of cold water, seasoned with the remaining salt, to a boil. Drop in the spaghetti one-third at a time. Stir once with a large kitchen fork and boil the spaghetti for about 8 minutes, or until just tender. Drain the spaghetti in a large colander, and shake it once or twice.

Slide the chicken livers into the hot sauce and simmer for a few seconds. Place the spaghetti in a large bowl, add the sauce, and toss. Serve immediately. No cheese, please.

$\mathscr{P}$ASTA $\mathscr{P}$RIMAVERA

If you wish to carry this recipe one step further, I suggest cooking the pasta in Chicken Stock (page 48) or in consommé. You will find it well worth the additional expenditure.

SERVES 4 TO 6

3 tablespoons olive oil
1 medium-sized onion, cut into thin slices
½ cup thinly sliced mushrooms
¼ cup very thin carrot strips
1 cup tiny broccoli florets, blanched
6 ripe tomatoes, blanched, seeded, and cut into ¼-inch-wide strips
2 tablespoons chopped fresh basil
4 thin slices prosciutto, cut into thin strips
1½ pounds spaghetti
2 tablespoons softened butter
1 cup grated imported Parmesan cheese

Heat the olive oil in a 10- or 12-inch skillet and cook the onion until transparent. Add the mushrooms, carrots, and broccoli and cook for 2 to 3 minutes, or until the mushrooms are soft. Remove from the heat, add the tomatoes, basil, and prosciutto, and set aside.

In a large pot, bring 6 to 8 quarts of salted water to a rolling boil. Drop in the spaghetti one-third at a time. Stir with a large kitchen fork and boil the spaghetti for 8 to 10 minutes. Taste for doneness. Drain the spaghetti in a large colander.

Melt the butter in the spaghetti pot. Return the spaghetti to the pot and toss it around in the butter. Immediately bring the sauce to a boil. Stirring constantly, mix the sauce into the pasta and serve on a large, heated platter with the Parmesan cheese.

$\mathscr{S}$PAGHETTI WITH $\mathscr{G}$ARLIC $\mathscr{S}$AUCE

This is one of those soul-warming quickies, especially when served with good Italian bread and the Tomato Salad on page 274.

SERVES 4

½ *cup olive oil*
2 *teaspoons finely chopped garlic*
4 *teaspoons salt*
6 *quarts water*
1 *pound spaghetti*
2 *tablespoons finely chopped flat-leaf parsley*
½ *cup freshly grated imported Parmesan cheese*

Combine the olive oil, garlic, and 1 teaspoon of salt in a small saucepan over medium heat, and when the garlic just starts to color, remove it from the heat.

In a large pot, bring 6 quarts of water to a boil with 1 tablespoon salt. Gradually add the spaghetti and stir with a large fork for a few minutes. Boil the spaghetti over high heat until just tender. Depending upon the thickness of the pasta, the cooking time could be from 6 to 10 minutes. The pasta should be resilient to the bite.

Drain the pasta in a large colander, shaking it over the sink to remove all the water. Wipe the pot dry with a paper towel and return the pasta to the pot. Quickly reheat the sauce and pour it over the pasta. Add the chopped parsley and stir with a long fork. Serve immediately on individual warm plates along with the grated cheese and a pepper mill.

Deep-Fried Rice Balls

Louis Maddaluno, proprietor of Zampagnaro Italian Specialty Food Store on Bleecker Street in Greenwich Village, was the inspiration for this recipe. On one of my many visits to this wonderful store, I found Louis shaping rice balls. Immediately we were engrossed in a lengthy conversation on how they should be made. Louis told me that in Sicily tomato is added to the rice mixture, an addition you might like to experiment with. The rice balls make a wonderful snack. Or they can be served at lunch, or even with cocktails. I prefer eating them while they are still warm and the cheese is stringy.

SERVES 6 TO 8

1 tablespoon butter
2 tablespoons finely chopped onion
1 cup long-grain rice
2½ cups fresh Chicken Stock (page 48) or canned broth
¼ pound mozzarella cheese, cut into ½-inch cubes
¼ pound grated Parmesan cheese
½ cup chopped prosciutto
¼ cup chopped flat-leaf parsley
1½ cups Fresh Bread Crumbs (page 12)
Vegetable oil for deep-fat frying

Melt the butter in a heavy 1-quart casserole, add the onion, and stir for about 2 minutes, until the onion is soft but not brown. Stir in the rice until each kernel glistens. Pour in the chicken stock and bring to a boil. Reduce the heat to low and cover tightly. Steam the rice for 20 minutes, until the grains are soft and have absorbed all the liquid. Dump the rice into a bowl and cool to room temperature.

Add the mozzarella and Parmesan cheese, the prosciutto, and parsley to the bowl of cooked rice. Shape the rice mixture into 2-inch balls. One at a time roll them in the bread crumbs.

256

Fill a large cast-iron skillet two-thirds full of vegetable oil. Using a deep-fat-frying thermometer, heat the oil to 375°.

Fry the rice balls 3 or 4 at a time, turning them frequently until they are golden brown. Remove them from the deep fat to a jelly roll pan lined with paper towels.

Serve hot or at room temperature.

GREEN RICE

This rice goes very well with any broiled fowl or fish. Because of the scallions and parsley, it should not be served with any sauced dish.

SERVES 6

4 tablespoons butter
1½ cups rice
1½ cups fresh Chicken Stock (page 48) or canned broth
½ cup thinly sliced scallions
¼ cup chopped flat-leaf parsley
Freshly ground black pepper to taste

Melt 1 tablespoon of the butter in a 1-quart saucepan. Add the rice and stir with a spoon until all the kernels glisten. Pour in the chicken stock, bring to a boil, reduce to a simmer, and cover. Steam the rice for 16 to 18 minutes, or until all of the chicken stock has been absorbed. Heat the remaining butter in a small skillet, add the scallions, and cook, stirring constantly, until the scallions just start to wilt. With a fork, stir the wilted scallions and the chopped parsley into the rice. Serve at once with a sprinkling of freshly ground black pepper.

$\mathscr{B}$ARLEY $\mathscr{C}$ASSEROLE

This casserole goes extremely well with any sauced meat or fowl.

SERVES 6

2 tablespoons butter
¼ cup finely chopped onion
1 cup medium pearled barley
3 cups fresh Chicken Stock (page 48) or canned broth
2 tablespoons finely chopped parsley

Heat the butter in a heavy 1-quart casserole. Add the onion and cook until transparent. Stir in the barley, add the chicken stock, bring to a boil, cover tightly, and cook over very low heat for 1 hour. Stir in the chopped parsley and serve.

$\mathscr{B}$UCKWHEAT $\mathscr{G}$ROATS WITH $\mathscr{P}$ECANS

This dish can replace rice or potatoes, or it makes a good stuffing for fowl.

SERVES 6

4 tablespoons unsalted butter
1 cup finely chopped onion
1 cup buckwheat groats
2 cups fresh Chicken Stock (page 48) or canned broth
½ cup shelled pecans
Salt and freshly ground black pepper to taste
2 tablespoons chopped parsley

Heat 2 tablespoons of the butter in a 1- or 1½-quart casserole, add the onion, and cook until transparent. Stir in the buckwheat groats, then add the chicken stock. Bring to a boil over high heat. Cover the casserole and cook for 20 to 30 minutes, or until the buckwheat groats have absorbed all the liquid and are tender. Remove from the heat and keep covered.

Heat the remaining butter in a small skillet and add the pecans, tossing them around in the hot butter for 2 to 3 minutes, or until they are toasted. Season the pecans with a little pepper and salt, then stir them into the buckwheat groats. Stir in the chopped parsley and serve.

LENTILS WITH COTECHINO SAUSAGE

These sausages can be found in any Italian pork shop. They can weigh from ¾ of a pound to 1¾ pounds, and they are approximately 2 inches in diameter.

This dish can also be served cold, with the addition of some vinaigrette, chopped flat-leaf parsley, and scallions.

SERVES 4 TO 6

One 1-to-1½-pound cotechino sausage
2 tablespoons butter
½ cup finely chopped onion
1 teaspoon finely chopped garlic
3 cups dried lentils, washed
1 bay leaf
3 cups water
½ teaspoon salt

Prick the sausage in several places with a large two-pronged kitchen fork. Place the sausage in a large saucepan and cover it with water. Bring the water to a boil, reduce the heat to a simmer, and cook the sausage for 45 minutes. Let the sausage cool in the liquid and, as soon as it is cool enough to handle, remove the skin.

Heat the butter in a 6- or 8-quart casserole and cook the onion and garlic until the onion is transparent. Stir in the lentils and the bay leaf, pour in the water, add the salt, and bring to a boil. Cover the pot and reduce the heat to a simmer. Cook the lentils for about 30 minutes or until they are tender. Slice the sausage into ½-inch rounds. When the lentils are tender, remove from the heat. Add the sausage slices, cover the casserole, and reheat for 5 minutes. Serve directly from the casserole.

261

$\mathscr{S}$ALADS

ARUGULA SALAD

This is one of my favorite salads to serve with Stuffed Veal Chops (page 141) and Chicken Breasts Milanaise Style (page 81).

SERVES 4

2 medium-sized bunches arugula
1 large clove garlic
4 tablespoons olive oil
4 teaspoons fresh lemon juice
¼ teaspoon salt
2 large, ripe tomatoes, blanched, peeled, seeded, and cut into ¼-inch-wide julienne strips
2 hard-boiled egg yolks

Trim the arugula of its tough stems and wash in cold water. Drain the arugula in a colander, then pat it dry with paper towels. Cut the clove of garlic in half and rub a salad bowl with the cut ends to release the garlic juice. Combine the olive oil, lemon juice, and salt in a small cup and beat with a dinner fork until the ingredients are well blended.

Place the arugula in the salad bowl, pour the dressing over the greens, and toss well. Add the strips of tomato and force the hard-boiled egg yolks through a fine sieve with the back of a wooden spoon over the salad. Toss again and serve with a pepper mill.

$\mathcal{A}$VOCADO AND $\mathcal{T}$OMATO $\mathcal{S}$ALAD

This salad can be served as a first course. It also goes well with grilled meats or Italian sausages. Another option is to mix 1 pound of small cooked shrimp into the salad to serve for a luncheon on crisp greens garnished with hard-cooked eggs.

SERVES 6

2 ripe avocados, peeled, cut into ½-inch pieces, and tossed with 1 tablespoon
   lemon juice
3 medium-sized tomatoes, blanched, peeled, seeded, and coarsely chopped
3 tablespoons grated onion
2 tablespoons chopped parsley
1½ teaspoons salt
Freshly ground black pepper to taste
2 tablespoons red wine vinegar
½ cup olive oil

In a medium-sized bowl combine the avocados, tomatoes, onion, parsley, and salt and pepper to taste. With a fork beat the vinegar and oil together and pour over the avocado-tomato mixture. Toss the ingredients together gently but thoroughly. Cover the bowl with plastic wrap and chill for at least 1 hour before serving.

ℬEAN 𝒮PROUT 𝒮ALAD

This salad also makes a nice lunch for three—or serve it stuffed in pita bread, as a sandwich.

SERVES 6

½ cup vegetable oil
3 tablespoons Japanese soy sauce
3 tablespoons sherry
3 tablespoons fresh lemon juice
½ teaspoon dry mustard
1 teaspoon grated fresh ginger
1 pound bean sprouts
¼ cup chopped scallions
2 large, ripe tomatoes, peeled, seeded, and chopped
2 tablespoons finely chopped cilantro
Salt and freshly ground black pepper to taste

Combine the oil, soy sauce, sherry, lemon juice, mustard, and ginger and set aside. In a large salad bowl, combine the bean sprouts, scallions, tomatoes, and cilantro.

Beat the oil mixture with a fork, blending all the ingredients well, pour over the salad mixture, and toss until all the salad is evenly coated with the dressing.

$\mathscr{S}$PICY $\mathscr{C}$AULIFLOWER $\mathscr{S}$ALAD

You can also serve broccoli in this manner, or, to double the number of servings, use both vegetables and double the dressing. If you prefer, replace the vegetable oil with olive oil.

SERVES 4

One 1-pound head of cauliflower
1 teaspoon salt
1 tablespoon finely chopped garlic
½ teaspoon Tabasco sauce
¼ cup distilled white vinegar
½ cup vegetable oil

With a sharp knife, cut away the base of the cauliflower and remove any green leaves. Gently separate the cauliflower into florets and set aside.

In a 2½- or 3-quart saucepan, bring 1 quart of water to a boil with ½ teaspoon of the salt. Drop in the florets, return the water to a boil, and cook uncovered for 8 minutes. Drain the cauliflower in a colander and set aside to cool.

In a large bowl combine the remaining salt, the garlic, Tabasco sauce, vinegar, and vegetable oil. Beat the mixture with a fork, drop in the cooked cauliflower, and toss until the cauliflower is completely coated with the dressing.

Refrigerate the Spicy Cauliflower Salad for 2 hours before serving.

𝒞UCUMBER 𝒮ALAD

Chinese sesame oil is this recipe's secret for success.

SERVES 4

4 medium-sized cucumbers, chilled
¾ teaspoon salt
6 tablespoons vegetable oil
2 tablespoons Chinese sesame oil
3 tablespoons distilled white vinegar
½ teaspoon dry mustard
2 tablespoons chopped chives

With a vegetable peeler, remove the skin from the cucumbers. Slice the cucumbers and, with a teaspoon, remove the seeds and discard. With a sharp knife slice the cucumbers crosswise into very thin slices. Place the cucumbers on a dinner plate and sprinkle them with ½ teaspoon of the salt. Cover with an inverted dinner plate and let the cucumbers chill in the refrigerator for at least 1 hour.

Remove the cucumbers from the refrigerator and, holding the plates in two hands, shake them over the sink to rid the cucumbers of their water. Place the cucumbers in a clean kitchen towel and squeeze them over the sink to rid them of any remaining water. Transfer the cucumbers to a salad bowl.

Combine the remaining salt, the vegetable oil, sesame oil, vinegar, and mustard, and with a dinner fork beat the ingredients until they are well blended.

Pour the dressing over the cucumbers and toss with the chives until the cucumbers are well coated with the dressing.

Cucumbers in Sour Cream

It is extremely important to remove the water from the cucumbers as instructed in the recipe; otherwise it will run into the sour cream dressing and turn the salad into a soupy mess.

This salad makes a nice accompaniment to fried or grilled fish.

SERVES 4 TO 6

4 medium-sized, firm cucumbers
2 teaspoons salt
1 cup sour cream
¼ cup distilled white vinegar
½ teaspoon sugar
¼ teaspoon white pepper
2 tablespoons finely chopped fresh dill

Scrape the peel from the cucumbers and slice them in half lengthwise. With a small spoon, scoop out the seeds and discard them.

Place the cucumber halves hollow side down on a chopping board and slice crosswise into very thin pieces. Place the sliced cucumbers in a colander, sprinkle with the salt, and toss them around with your fingers. Let the cucumbers sit for at least 30 minutes.

Put the sour cream in a mixing bowl and beat in the white vinegar, sugar, white pepper, and dill and set aside.

Place half the sliced cucumbers in a clean kitchen towel and squeeze out the water.* Add the cucumbers to the sour cream and repeat with the remaining sliced cucumbers. Combine the cucumbers thoroughly with the sour cream dressing. Cover with plastic wrap and refrigerate for at least 2 hours before serving.

* It is extremely important to squeeze the cucumbers very tightly to extract all their water. When you open the towel the cucumber slices should look opaque. Remember that the firmer the cucumber, the fresher it is, which means it contains a great amount of water.

COLE SLAW

The slaw will be perfectly good after 2 hours of refrigeration, but I prefer to make it the day before—the cabbage gets a little wilted, and the slaw becomes creamier.

SERVES 6 TO 8

2½ pounds cabbage
1 cup Mayonnaise (page 294)
1 cup sour cream
1 teaspoon sugar
2 teaspoons dry mustard
2 tablespoons chopped chives
2 teaspoons celery salt
1 teaspoon salt
Freshly ground white pepper to taste

Remove and discard the outer bruised leaves and with a large knife cut the cabbage into quarters through the core. Cut the core away from the leaves. With a large knife or a food processor, shred the cabbage very thin and place it in a large bowl.

Combine the mayonnaise, sour cream, sugar, dry mustard, chopped chives, celery salt, salt, and white pepper in a medium-sized bowl. Beat the ingredients until they are well blended. Stir the dressing into the shredded cabbage. Cover with plastic wrap and refrigerate for at least 2 hours before serving.

ENDIVE AND
WATERCRESS SALAD

*Many people are allergic to walnut oil, so unless you know your
guests well, replace the walnut oil with a top-grade olive oil.*

SERVES 4

2 *large heads endive*
1 *large bunch watercress*
3 *tablespoons walnut oil*
1 *tablespoon sherry wine vinegar*
¼ *teaspoon dry mustard*
Salt and freshly ground black pepper to taste

Wash the endive and watercress under cold water and pat dry with
paper towels. Core the endive and slice into thin, long strips. Cut the stems
from the watercress and place the greens in a salad bowl.

Mix the oil, vinegar, dry mustard, salt, and pepper in a small mixing
bowl. Beat the ingredients with a dinner fork, then pour the dressing over
the greens and toss well.

$\mathcal{T}$OMATO $\mathcal{A}$SPIC

This Tomato Aspic will go well with the Mock Fried Chicken Breasts on page 84. If you wish to serve a sauce with the aspic, mix 2 tablespoons milk with 1 cup sour cream and add 1/4 cup chopped chives. Adding chopped cucumbers is another nice touch.

SERVES 6

2 envelopes unflavored gelatin
1/2 cup cold water mixed with 1 tablespoon Worcestershire sauce
1/2 cup finely chopped onion
1/4 cup finely chopped celery, with some leaves
4 cups canned tomatoes with their juices
3/4 teaspoon salt
1/2 teaspoon sugar
1 teaspoon dried tarragon, crumbled
1 1/2 teaspoons vegetable oil

Soften the gelatin in the cold water and Worcestershire sauce. In a heavy 2½- or 3-quart saucepan combine the onion, celery, tomatoes, salt, sugar, and tarragon. With your hands, carefully crush the tomatoes. Bring the mixture to a boil, reduce the heat to very low, and simmer partially covered for 30 minutes. Pass the mixture through a food mill into a bowl and set it aside to cool to room temperature. With a paper towel, lightly coat the inside of a 6-cup ring mold with the vegetable oil. Pour the cooled tomato mixture into the mold and refrigerate for 3 hours, or until the aspic is set.

When ready to serve the aspic, place a serving plate on top of the mold and invert the two. Tap the mold and the aspic should slide out onto the plate. If it does not, rub the outside of the mold with a hot towel to loosen the aspic.

TOMATO SALAD

This is probably the most seasonal recipe in this book. It should be made only with vine-ripened tomatoes. Don't waste expensive olive oil on the "plastic" tomatoes sold out of season.

SERVES 4

4 beefsteak tomatoes, blanched and peeled
1 red onion, sliced very thin
Salt and freshly ground black pepper to taste
6 tablespoons olive oil
2 tablespoons red wine vinegar
¼ cup chopped flat-leaf parsley
¼ cup chopped fresh basil, or 1 tablespoon dried basil, crumbled

Cut the stem end from each tomato. Slice the tomatoes ½ inch thick. Arrange on a shallow serving dish alternating with the sliced red onion. Season with salt and pepper. Mix the oil and vinegar together and dribble over the tomato and onion. Sprinkle with the parsley and basil and serve.

GERMAN POTATO SALAD

This salad is perfect for anyone who does not care for mayonnaise.

SERVES 6 TO 8

3 pounds small new potatoes
½ cup finely chopped celery
1 cup finely chopped onion
1½ cups vegetable oil
¼ cup distilled white vinegar
1½ teaspoons salt
1 egg yolk
¼ teaspoon freshly ground white pepper
¼ cup chopped parsley

Place the potatoes in a large pot and cover with cold water. Bring the water to a boil over high heat and cook the potatoes for 10 minutes. Test for doneness by piercing the potatoes with the point of a paring knife. Drain the potatoes in a colander and, when they are cool enough to handle, peel them and cut them into ¼-inch-thick slices. Place the potatoes, celery, and onion in a large bowl and mix well.

Combine the vegetable oil, vinegar, salt, egg yolk, pepper, and parsley. Beat the ingredients with a fork, pour over the potato mixture, and mix well. Cover with plastic wrap and refrigerate for at least 2 hours before serving.

White Bean and Tuna Salad

This recipe is of Italian origin, and the white kidney beans are called cannellini. If you are short on time you can buy canned cannellini and rinse them under cold water before proceeding with the recipe.

SERVES 4 TO 6

2 cups dried white kidney beans
1½ teaspoons salt
½ cup olive oil
2 tablespoons fresh lemon juice
2 large tomatoes, blanched, peeled, seeded, and coarsely chopped
¼ cup finely chopped scallions
¼ cup finely chopped flat-leaf parsley
Two 7-ounce cans tuna fish, packed in olive oil
Freshly ground black pepper to taste

Combine the beans and enough cold water to cover in a large, heavy casserole. Add 1 teaspoon of the salt and bring the liquid to a boil. Cover the casserole and cook the beans for 2 minutes. Remove from the heat and soak the beans, still covered, for 1 hour. Return the beans to high heat and bring to a boil, lower the heat, and simmer for 1½ hours.

Mix the olive oil, lemon juice, and remaining salt together. When the beans are tender, drain them thoroughly in a colander. Drop the beans into a large serving bowl and immediately stir in the olive oil mixture. Cool the mixture to room temperature, then add the tomatoes, scallions, parsley, and tuna fish, broken into small pieces. Mix all the ingredients well, season with salt and pepper, and cover with plastic wrap. Chill in the refrigerator for 2 hours before serving.

CHICKEN SALAD

Besides adding flavor, the sour cream makes for a much lighter dressing. Arranging slices of tomato, hard-boiled egg, and cucumber spears around the platter makes a colorful frame for the salad.

SERVES 6 TO 8

6 cups cooked chicken, cut into ½-inch pieces
1½ teaspoons salt
Freshly ground black pepper to taste
6 tablespoons chopped onion
½ cup finely chopped celery
1¼ cups fresh Mayonnaise (page 294) }
1¼ cups sour cream   } *mixed together*
2 tablespoons finely chopped parsley

Place the chicken pieces in a large mixing bowl. Sprinkle with the salt and pepper to taste. Add the onion and celery. Toss together, then add the mayonnaise–sour cream mixture. Combine all ingredients thoroughly. Allow the salad to rest for 2 hours in the refrigerator before serving.

Just before serving, taste for seasoning. Serve the salad on a large lettuce-lined platter and sprinkle with parsley.

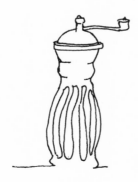

CHICKEN IN ORANGE ASPIC

For additional flavor and a refreshing color change, I often add ½ cup of cooked whole cranberries to the chicken mixture.

SERVES 6

CHICKEN

One 4-pound roasting chicken, cut into quarters
Chicken giblets
4 cups fresh orange juice; reserve the rind
4 cups fresh Chicken Stock (page 48) or canned broth
1½ cups chopped onion
½ cup chopped carrot
¾ cup chopped celery, plus some leaves

ORANGE ASPIC

Reserved chicken stock
3 envelopes unflavored gelatin
¾ cup cold water
Reserved rind of 1 orange, coarsely chopped
3 egg whites, beaten to a froth
3 egg shells, crushed

Salt and freshly ground black pepper to taste
2 tablespoons chopped parsley
2 tablespoons grated orange rind

TO COOK THE CHICKEN

Place the chicken and the giblets in a large pot. Add the orange juice and the chicken stock. Bring to a boil and skim off the foam from the

278

surface, then add the onion, carrot, and celery. If the liquid does not cover the chicken completely, add more stock. Reduce the heat to a simmer and cook the chicken, partially covered, for 1 hour to 1 hour and 15 minutes, or until the chicken is tender.

Remove the chicken from the pot and reserve the stock. When the chicken is cool enough to handle, remove the skin and cut the meat away from the bones. Discard the bones. Cover the meat with plastic wrap and refrigerate.

TO MAKE THE ORANGE ASPIC

Strain the chicken stock through a fine sieve and skim all fat from the surface. Measure 4 cups of the stock for the aspic. (Reserve any leftover stock for future use.)

Soften the gelatin in the cold water, then stir it into the stock. Add the chopped orange rind, beaten egg whites, and egg shells. Set the pan over high heat and, stirring constantly, bring to a boil. Reduce the heat to low and simmer the stock for 10 minutes undisturbed.

Strain the stock through a cheesecloth-lined sieve into a bowl. Allow the stock to drain without disturbing it.

TO ASSEMBLE THE CHICKEN IN ORANGE ASPIC

Remove the chicken meat from the refrigerator and cut it into 1-inch squares, season with a little salt and pepper, then add the chopped parsley and grated orange rind.

Rinse a 2-quart mixing bowl (stainless steel is the best) with cold water. Pour the aspic into the bowl and set it in a larger bowl of crushed ice.

Stir very gently with a metal spoon until the aspic becomes a thick syrup. Then mix in the seasoned chicken meat. Refrigerate for about 3 hours, or until the aspic is set.

When ready to serve, dip the bottom of the bowl into hot water, then wipe it dry. Invert the bowl on a large, chilled platter. Quickly turn the bowl and the platter over and firmly place it on the table to unmold. If you are not serving this dish immediately, return it to the refrigerator.

$\mathcal{H}$ERRING $\mathcal{S}$ALAD

Piled on crisp lettuce leaves and served with Parker House Rolls (page 304), this Herring Salad makes a wonderful lunch. You wouldn't believe what an apple can do for a herring.

SERVES 6 TO 8

2 hard-cooked eggs, coarsely chopped
4 medium-sized beets, boiled
4 medium-sized potatoes, boiled and cut into ½-inch dice
1 Matjis herring
½ pound boiled beef, cut into ½-inch dice
½ pound cooked ham, cut into ½-inch dice
1 red Delicious apple, cored and cut into ½-inch dice
2 sour dill pickles
2 tablespoons dry mustard
1½ teaspoons sugar
1½ cups sour cream

In a large bowl, combine the eggs, beets, potatoes, herring, boiled beef, ham, and apple. Chop the dill pickles. Place in a clean kitchen towel and wring the juice out. Add the pickle to the bowl, along with the mustard, sugar, and sour cream, and mix well.

Sauces

CLARIFIED BUTTER

Clarified butter is the same as drawn butter. It is simply melted butter with the water and milky sediment removed, leaving clear butter fat. The result is a cooking butter that has a much higher smoke point.

MAKES ABOUT 12 TABLESPOONS

½ *pound unsalted butter*

Melt the butter in a small, heavy saucepan over very low heat. Pour the melted butter into a 2-cup glass heatproof measure. In a few minutes the milky solids will settle to the bottom. Carefully spoon out the clear butter and pour into a small container.

COLD AVOCADO SAUCE

Do not be concerned about the sour cream curdling as you bring it to a boil—the arrowroot will stabilize the sour cream.

This sauce goes well with cold fish or shellfish, and if you thin it with a little heavy cream, it makes a very good dip for raw vegetables.

MAKES ABOUT 2½ CUPS

1 large, very ripe avocado
2 tablespoons fresh lemon juice
1 teaspoon finely chopped garlic
1 tablespoon arrowroot
¼ cup water
1 cup sour cream
2 tablespoons chopped chives
Salt and freshly ground black pepper to taste

Mash the avocado with the lemon juice and garlic in a medium-sized bowl. Mix in the arrowroot, water, sour cream, and chives. Scrape the mixture into a small saucepan and bring to a boil over high heat. Remove from the heat and transfer the sauce to a small, clean bowl. Cover with plastic wrap and chill for at least 2 hours. Before serving taste for salt and pepper.

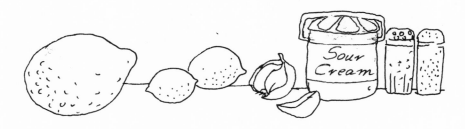

BARBECUE SAUCE

For a smoother sauce, purée it through a food mill. Covered tightly the sauce will keep for a week or more in the refrigerator.

MAKES ABOUT 2 CUPS

¼ cup vegetable oil
1½ cups finely chopped onions
¼ cup dark brown sugar
¼ cup distilled white vinegar
¼ cup Worcestershire sauce
2 teaspoons dry mustard
½ teaspoon Tabasco sauce
½ cup chili sauce
¼ cup apricot preserves
1 cup water

Heat the vegetable oil in a heavy 1-quart saucepan. Add the onions and cook until they just start to brown. Remove from the heat and stir in the brown sugar, white vinegar, Worcestershire sauce, mustard, Tabasco sauce, chili sauce, and apricot preserves. Stir the mixture until all the ingredients are thoroughly mixed and smooth. Gradually add the water, return the saucepan to the heat, and bring the mixture to a boil. Reduce the heat to low and cook the Barbecue Sauce uncovered for 15 minutes.

$\mathscr{S}$AUCE $\mathscr{B}$OLOGNESE

Good pastas to serve with this sauce are mostacciole, green noodles, and rigatoni. If 4 cups is more than you need, the leftovers can be frozen for several months.

MAKES ABOUT 4 CUPS

4 tablespoons butter
¼ pound ground or finely chopped prosciutto
1½ cups finely chopped onion
¼ cup finely chopped carrot
¾ cup finely chopped celery
1½ pounds finely ground shin of beef
½ pound finely ground lean pork
1 cup dry white wine
¼ cup tomato paste
1 quart fresh Chicken Stock (page 48), or canned broth
1½ cups heavy cream
¼ teaspoon ground nutmeg
Salt and freshly ground black pepper to taste

Heat the butter in a heavy 2- or 3-quart casserole. Add the prosciutto, onion, carrot, and celery. Cook the mixture until the onion is lightly browned. Add the ground beef and pork and cook gently until there is no trace of pink. Do not allow the meat to brown. Add the wine, increase the heat, and boil until the liquid has cooked away. Stir in the tomato paste and stock and simmer partially covered for 1 hour. Stir in the cream; add the nutmeg and salt and pepper to taste.

Basic Brown Sauce

There is nothing more frustrating than wanting to cook something and finding that the recipe calls for 1 cup of Basic Brown Sauce.

You can easily double this recipe if you want to keep some sauce on hand for just such an occasion. The Basic Brown Sauce will keep nicely in your freezer for several months. Using this recipe you can make an almost endless number of other sauces.

MAKES 2 CUPS

2 cups fresh Beef Stock (page 46)
2 large mushrooms, chopped
3 scallions, chopped
2 sprigs parsley
3 tablespoons arrowroot mixed with ¼ cup cold water

In a heavy 1-quart saucepan combine the stock, mushrooms, scallions, and parsley. Slowly bring the stock to a simmer, reduce the heat to low, and cook uncovered for 15 minutes. Give the arrowroot and water a stir and very gently whisk it into the sauce. Simmer the sauce for an additional 2 to 3 minutes. Strain the sauce through a fine sieve.

$\mathscr{S}$ALSA $\mathscr{C}$RUDA

Served with tortilla chips or grilled meats, Salsa Cruda has a fresh, mouthwatering flavor.

MAKES ABOUT 1½ CUPS

4 medium-sized tomatoes, peeled, seeded, and finely chopped
One 4-ounce can of green chilies, seeded and finely chopped
2 tablespoons chopped cilantro
½ cup finely chopped onion
2 tablespoons sherry wine vinegar
1½ teaspoons sugar
Salt to taste

In a medium-sized bowl combine the tomatoes, chilies, cilantro, onion, sherry wine vinegar, and sugar. Mix well. Taste for seasoning; you may want to add a little salt.

Let the sauce rest at room temperature for at least 30 minutes before serving.

ᴹUSTARD ᴾAUCE

This mustard sauce is a good complement to steamed or poached fish. You might like to try it with boiled beef; if so, eliminate the fish stock.

MAKES ABOUT 2 CUPS

¼ cup Dijon mustard
1 tablespoon arrowroot
4 tablespoons softened butter
4 egg yolks
1 cup fresh Chicken, Beef, or Fish Stock (pages 48, 46, 45)
1 tablespoon fresh lemon juice
1 teaspoon Worcestershire sauce
¼ teaspoon sugar

Put the mustard in a small, heavy saucepan and with a wire whisk beat in the arrowroot, butter, egg yolks, and stock. Whisk constantly over high heat until the mixture thickens. Remove from the heat and stir in the lemon juice, Worcestershire sauce, and sugar.

289

*S*auce *N*antua

*This sauce can be used with any poached white fish and goes well
with the Mousse of Sea Scallops on page 174.*

SERVES 6 TO 8

*6 medium-sized shrimp in their shells
9 tablespoons unsalted butter
½ cup Fish Stock (page 45)
4 tablespoons all-purpose flour
1 cup light cream
⅛ teaspoon dried thyme
1 teaspoon salt
⅛ teaspoon cayenne pepper
1 tablespoon tomato paste
Salt and freshly ground black pepper to taste*

Chop the shrimp, shells and all, into ½-inch pieces. Heat 6 table-spoons of the butter in a small skillet. Cook the shrimp in the butter until the shells turn pink and the flesh feels firm. Scrape the contents of the skillet into the container of a food processor and process the shrimp until it is completely pulverized. Scrape the shrimp and butter mixture into a fine sieve set over a medium-sized bowl. With the back of a wooden spoon, push the mixture through the sieve. Discard the solids. Blend the fish stock with the shrimp essence.

Melt the remaining 3 tablespoons of butter in a small saucepan, add the flour, and cook over low heat for about 2 minutes. Remove the saucepan from the heat and slowly whisk in the cream. Add the thyme, salt, and cayenne, return the mixture to the heat, and let it come to a boil.

Reduce the heat and simmer the sauce for 2 minutes. Beat in the shrimp essence and tomato paste; taste for salt and pepper.

$\mathscr{S}$PICED $\mathscr{P}$ARSLEY $\mathscr{S}$AUCE

This fresh-tasting sauce goes very well with poached fish and boiled or broiled meats.

MAKES ABOUT 2 CUPS

1 cup olive oil
½ cup sherry wine vinegar
½ cup very finely chopped onion
1½ teaspoons garlic
1½ teaspoons oregano
2 teaspoons salt
1½ teaspoons freshly ground black pepper
½ cup freshly chopped flat-leaf parsley

Measure and mix all the above ingredients together in a medium-sized bowl. Cover with plastic wrap and refrigerate overnight.

Remove from refrigerator at least 2 hours before serving.

ᴾizza ᴼauce

*This sauce does not have to be used only for pizza. By adding mush-
rooms, Italian sausage, shrimp, or clams, you can have a simple, quick sauce
for pasta. Adding a bit of chopped flat-leaf parsley will enhance the flavor
even further.*

MAKES ABOUT 4 CUPS

4 tablespoons olive oil
1½ cups finely chopped onion
1 tablespoon finely chopped garlic
4 cups canned tomatoes, with their liquid
6 tablespoons tomato paste
2 teaspoons dried oregano
2 teaspoons dried basil
1 tablespoon salt

Heat the olive oil in a 4-quart casserole and cook the onion and garlic
until the onion is transparent. Pour in the liquid from the canned tomatoes.
Put the tomatoes in a large bowl and crush them with your hands. Add
them to the contents of the casserole. Stir in the tomato paste, oregano,
basil, and salt. Bring the liquid to a boil and reduce the heat to low. Simmer
the sauce, partially covered, for 1 hour. Purée the sauce through a food mill
fitted with a medium-sized blade.

HOLLANDAISE SAUCE

The technique used to make this sauce is called the direct heat method. It is much quicker than using a double boiler, and I personally prefer it to using a blender or food processor.

MAKES ABOUT 2 CUPS

4 egg yolks
1 tablespoon cold water
2 tablespoons lemon juice
½ teaspoon salt
⅛ teaspoon cayenne pepper
½ pound unsalted butter, melted

In a small, heavy saucepan (not aluminum), mix all the above ingredients except the butter. Place the saucepan on the lowest possible heat and with a wire whisk beat the ingredients until the bottom of the pan shows through when the whisk is drawn across it. Remove the saucepan from the heat. Add the hot butter about ¼ cup at a time, beating well after each addition. When all the butter has been incorporated, the sauce will be thick enough to hold its shape on a spoon.

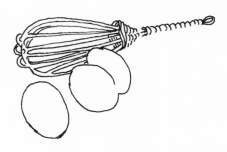

ℳAYONNAISE

There is nothing wrong with having a jar of good quality mayonnaise in your refrigerator for a quick sandwich. But for that special recipe, make your own—you will notice a big difference.

MAKES ABOUT 2 CUPS

3 egg yolks, at room temperature
1 teaspoon prepared mustard
½ teaspoon salt
⅛ teaspoon cayenne pepper
1½ cups olive oil
1 tablespoon fresh lemon juice

Place the egg yolks, mustard, salt, and cayenne pepper in the container of a food processor or electric mixer. Beat the mixture on high speed for 2 to 3 minutes. At medium speed add the olive oil in a very fine stream. After 1 cup of the oil has been incorporated, the remainder can be added more rapidly. Beat in the lemon juice, cover with plastic wrap, and refrigerate for at least 2 hours before using.

$\mathcal{T}$ARTAR $\mathcal{S}$AUCE

I prefer the dill pickles that are sold loose. In a pinch, use ½ cup of pickle relish and add a little lemon juice or vinegar to compensate for the sweetness of the relish.

MAKES ABOUT 3 CUPS

½ cup finely chopped dill pickles
2 cups fresh Mayonnaise (page 294)
½ cup grated onion
1 tablespoon finely chopped parsley
½ teaspoon salt
⅛ teaspoon cayenne pepper

Place the chopped dill pickles in a clean kitchen towel and squeeze out the juices. Combine the pickles, mayonnaise, onion, parsley, salt, and pepper in a medium-sized bowl. Mix well and refrigerate, covered with plastic wrap, for at least 2 hours before serving.

Almond Custard Sauce

This light custard can be served with poached pears or plain Sponge Cake (page 315) and goes very well with Chocolate Mousse (page 336).

MAKES ABOUT 1½ CUPS

1½ cups milk
1 tablespoon cornstarch mixed with 2 tablespoons water
4 teaspoons sugar
1 egg yolk
½ teaspoon almond extract

Combine the milk, cornstarch and water, and the sugar in a small, heavy saucepan. Cook the mixture, stirring with a wooden spoon, until it comes to a boil and thickens. Beat the egg yolk in a small cup with 3 tablespoons of the hot sauce, then stir the mixture back into the saucepan. Return to a boil, remove from the heat, and stir in the almond extract. Pour the Almond Custard Sauce into a storage container and refrigerate.

BREADS, PIES, CAKES, AND OTHER DESSERTS

Yorkshire Popovers

Obviously this is the same recipe as Yorkshire pudding. Often I cook the mixture in a pudding dish. But for a nice presentation, cook the popovers in cupcake tins and pile them around a rib roast.

MAKES 8 POPOVERS

2 eggs
1 cup milk
1 cup all-purpose flour
½ teaspoon salt
6 tablespoons roast beef drippings

PREHEAT THE OVEN TO 425°F

Beat the eggs in a large bowl with a wire whisk. Gradually add the milk and then the flour, salt, and 3 tablespoons of the roast beef drippings. Continue to beat the batter until it is smooth. Grease an 8-cup muffin tin with the remaining drippings. Fill each cup two-thirds full. Bake the popovers on the middle shelf of the oven for 15 minutes. Reduce the heat to 375° and bake about 15 minutes longer, or until the popovers are a deep crusty brown. Serve immediately.

CHEESE BREAD

This is one of my favorite breads. It is good toasted and served with sweet butter, and it also makes very good croutons for soups or salads.

MAKES 2 LOAVES

2 envelopes active dry yeast
½ teaspoon sugar
½ cup warm water (110° to 115°F)
8 cups all-purpose flour
2½ teaspoons salt
1½ teaspoons cayenne pepper
2 cups milk, scalded, then cooled to 110° to 115°F
6 eggs
2½ cups grated sharp cheddar cheese
2 egg yolks, beaten

Add the yeast and sugar to the warm water and stir. Set the mixture aside until it doubles in volume, about 4 to 6 minutes.

Place the flour, salt, and cayenne in a large mixing bowl. Using a large wooden spoon, mix the dry ingredients together. Pour in the milk, yeast mixture, eggs, and grated cheese. Continue to stir with the wooden spoon until the flour has absorbed all the liquid.

With your hands, gather the dough and shape it into a ball. Place the ball of dough on a clean, lightly floured surface and knead it for 10 minutes. If the dough sticks to the surface, add more flour until the dough no longer sticks as you knead it. When the dough is shiny and silky to your touch, shape it into a ball.

Grease the inside of a large mixing bowl with a tablespoon of butter. Roll the ball of dough in the bowl to coat the entire surface with butter. Cover the dough with a towel and let rise for 1½ hours. After 1½ hours the dough should be double in volume. To test whether the dough has risen enough, press two fingertips into the surface. If the indentations remain, it is ready.

Punch the dough down and knead it for a few minutes. Cover with the towel and let rise for 1 hour and 15 minutes.

Grease the inside of two 9 x 5 x 5-inch bread pans. When the dough has risen the second time, turn it out onto your work surface. With the palms of your hands, flatten the dough to decrease the volume and shape it into a rectangle. With the handle of a wooden spoon, cut the dough into two equal pieces. Shape both pieces into loaves and place them in the prepared pans. Brush the tops of the loaves with the beaten egg yolks. Cover with a towel and let the loaves rise for 45 minutes, or until the center of the dough reaches the top of the pan.

PREHEAT THE OVEN TO 375°F

When the dough has risen, brush again with the egg yolks. Place the pans on the middle shelf of the preheated oven and bake for 45 minutes.

To test for doneness, remove the bread from the pan and tap the sides of the loaf with your knuckles. If it sounds hollow, the bread is done. If not, return it to the oven and bake for an additional 10 minutes.

Cool the loaves to room temperature on wire racks before cutting or storing.

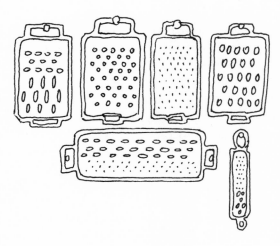

CROISSANTS

Because they have become so popular in the past few years, many companies package very good croissants. If for any reason they are not available to you, try this recipe. Although time-consuming, it will be fun and well worth the effort.

MAKES 3 DOZEN

2 *teaspoons active dry yeast*
1½ *cups warm water (110° to 115°F)*
A pinch of sugar, plus ¼ cup
4 *cups flour*
2 *teaspoons salt*
½ *cup milk*
½ *pound unsalted butter, softened*
½ *cup heavy cream*

Add the yeast to ½ cup of the water, then add the pinch of sugar and stir the mixture together. Set aside; the yeast will soon begin to foam. Place the flour in a large mixing bowl. Add the salt, the milk, and the remaining water and sugar. Stir in the yeast mixture. With a wooden spoon stir all the ingredients together until they are well blended. Cover the bowl and chill the dough for 1 hour.

Shape the butter into two rectangles measuring about 6 x 4 inches each. Wrap in wax paper and place in the refrigerator to chill. Remove the dough from the refrigerator, and on a lightly floured surface roll it into a rectangle measuring about 12 x 22 inches. Place one rectangle of the chilled butter across the center of the dough and bring the end of the dough farthest from you over the butter. Place the other rectangle of butter on top and bring the other half of the dough over that, sealing along the sides with your fingers. Wrap in foil and place in the refrigerator for 20 minutes.

Remove the dough from the refrigerator, unwrap it, and place it on a lightly floured surface with the narrow open end facing you. Roll it out just as you did before. Dust off any excess flour on the surface of the dough and fold it into three layers. Wrap it in foil and return it to the refrigerator to chill and rest for 20 minutes. Repeat the rolling and folding three more times. After the last folding return the dough to the refrigerator to chill and rest for 4 to 5 hours or overnight.

To shape the croissants, cut the dough in half and return half to the refrigerator. Roll the other half into a long strip 5½ inches wide and ⅛ inch thick. Using a croissant cutter, cut the dough and place the cut pieces on a cookie sheet, separating the layers with wax paper. Repeat this procedure with the second half of the dough. One at a time, shape the croissants by rolling from the wide end, stretching as you roll toward the point. Place them on an ungreased cookie sheet, brush them with the heavy cream, and allow them to rise at room temperature until they double in size. This will take about 1½ hours.

PREHEAT THE OVEN TO 400°F

Brush the croissants again with the cream and bake them in the preheated oven for 8 minutes; reduce the heat to 350° and bake for 10 to 12 minutes longer. Cool the croissants on a wire cake rack.

$\mathscr{P}$ARKER $\mathscr{H}$OUSE $\mathscr{R}$OLLS

These rolls were the specialty of the old Parker House Hotel in Boston. Easy to make, they work well for a large buffet of American fare.

MAKES ABOUT 24 ROLLS

1 envelope active dry yeast
4 teaspoons sugar
½ cup warm water (110° to 115°F)
4 to 5 cups all-purpose flour
1 teaspoon salt
1½ cups milk
1 egg, lightly beaten
2 tablespoons softened butter
3 tablespoons melted butter

Add the yeast and ½ teaspoon of the sugar to the warm water and stir. Set the mixture aside for 4 to 6 minutes, or until it has doubled in volume.

Place 4 cups of the flour, the remaining sugar, the salt, milk, egg, softened butter, and yeast mixture into a large mixing bowl. Stir the ingredients with a large wooden spoon until the flour has absorbed all the liquid. With your hands, gather the dough and shape it into a ball. Place the ball of dough on a clean, lightly floured surface and knead it for 10 minutes. If the dough sticks to the surface, add more flour as needed. When the dough is shiny and silky to the touch, shape it into a ball.

Using a little butter, grease the inside of a large mixing bowl. Roll the ball of dough in the bowl to coat the entire surface with butter. Cover the bowl with a towel and let the dough rise for 1 hour. After 1 hour the dough should be doubled in volume. To test whether it has risen enough, press two fingertips into the surface. If the indentations remain it is ready.

Turn the dough out onto the work surface and roll it out to ¼ inch thick. Cut the dough into 3-inch rounds with a cookie cutter. Gather the scraps and continue to roll and cut until all the dough has been shaped.

Make a deep crease with the back side of a dinner knife 1 inch from the edge of the dough. Fold the smaller side of the dough over the larger side and gently press down the edges.

PREHEAT THE OVEN TO 450°F

Place the rolls 1 inch apart on cookie sheets lined with parchment paper. Brush them with the melted butter and let them rise for 30 minutes, or until they double in size.

Bake the rolls in the preheated oven for 12 to 15 minutes, or until they are golden brown. Cool the Parker House Rolls on wire racks.

White Bread

It would be mind-boggling to say the least to learn how many loaves of commercial white bread are consumed each year in this country. Every time I make white bread, I can't help thinking of all the unfortunate people who have never tasted or experienced the wonderful flavor and tight texture of homemade bread.

It takes no longer to make two loaves. Store one in the freezer for future use.

MAKES 2 LOAVES

2 envelopes active dry yeast
½ teaspoon sugar
1 cup warm water (110° to 115°F)
6 cups all-purpose flour
1 tablespoon salt
1½ cups milk
6 tablespoons unsalted butter, softened
2 whole eggs, beaten, for glazing the bread

Add the yeast and sugar to the warm water and stir. Set the mixture aside until it doubles in volume.

Place the flour and the salt in a large mixing bowl. Using a large wooden spoon, mix the dry ingredients together. Pour in the milk, the yeast mixture, and the butter. Continue to stir with the wooden spoon until the flour has absorbed all the liquid.

With your hands, gather the dough and shape it into a ball. Place the ball of dough on a lightly floured surface and knead it for 10 minutes. If the dough sticks to the surface, add more flour as needed. When the dough is shiny and silky to the touch, shape it into a ball.

Using a little butter, grease the inside of a large bowl. Roll the ball of dough in the bowl to coat the entire surface with butter. Cover the bowl with a towel and let the dough rise for 1 hour. After 1 hour, the dough should be doubled in volume. To test it, press two fingertips into the surface; if the indentations remain the dough has risen enough.

Punch the dough down and knead it for a few minutes. Cover with the towel and let the dough rise for 1 hour and 15 minutes.

Grease the insides of two 9 x 5 x 5-inch bread pans. When the dough has risen for the second time, turn it out onto your work surface. With the palms of your hands, flatten the dough to decrease the volume and shape it into a rectangle.

With the handle of a wooden spoon, cut the dough into two equal pieces. Shape both pieces into loaves and place them in the prepared pans. Brush the tops of the loaves with the beaten egg. Cover with a towel and let the loaves rise for 45 minutes, or until the center of the dough reaches the top of the pan.

PREHEAT THE OVEN TO 375°F

When the dough has risen, brush the loaves again with the beaten egg. Place the pans on the middle shelf of the preheated oven and bake for 45 minutes.

To test for doneness, remove the bread from the pan and tap the sides of the loaves with your knuckles.

If it sounds hollow, the bread is done. If not, return it to the oven for an additional 10 minutes.

Cool the loaves to room temperature on wire racks before cutting or storing.

𝒮KILLET 𝒞ORNBREAD

The golden brown cornbread framed by the black iron pan makes an attractive picture. Keep a clean pot holder on the handle of the skillet as a reminder that it's hot. If you would like a perfect American dinner, serve Skillet Cornbread with Fried Chicken (page 79) and Pennsylvania Dutch Fried Tomatoes (page 231).

MAKES ONE 10-INCH ROUND LOAF

6 tablespoons butter plus 1 tablespoon for greasing the skillet
6 tablespoons vegetable shortening
1¾ cups yellow cornmeal
¾ cup all-purpose flour
⅓ cup sugar
1 teaspoon salt
1 tablespoon double-acting baking powder
3 eggs, lightly beaten
1¼ cups milk

PREHEAT THE OVEN TO 400°F

Melt 6 tablespoons of the butter and the vegetable shortening in a small saucepan and set aside to cool. Sift together into a mixing bowl the cornmeal, flour, sugar, salt, and baking powder. Add the eggs, milk, and cooled butter and shortening. Stir the mixture with a wooden spoon just until the batter is smooth. Do not overbeat. Grease a 10-inch iron skillet with the remaining 1 tablespoon of butter. Pour the cornbread batter into the skillet and bake on the middle shelf of the oven for 25 to 30 minutes, or until the cornbread shrinks slightly away from the sides of the skillet. Serve warm from the skillet.

CHOCOLATE CHIP COOKIES

Chocolate chip cookies have made a few people very rich in the last ten years or so. Good or bad, you can buy them almost anywhere. These are the chocolate chip cookies I knew as a child and still love as much now as I did then.

MAKES 36 COOKIES

12 tablespoons unsalted butter plus 2 tablespoons for greasing the pans
½ cup granulated sugar
½ cup dark brown sugar
¾ teaspoon pure vanilla extract
2 eggs
1½ cups all-purpose flour
½ teaspoon salt
1 teaspoon baking soda
¾ cup semisweet chocolate bits
¾ cup chopped pecans or walnuts

PREHEAT THE OVEN TO 375°F

In an electric mixer, combine the 12 tablespoons of butter, the granulated and brown sugars, and the vanilla, and beat them together until light and creamy. Beat in the eggs one at a time until they are well incorporated. Place a sifter on a piece of wax paper. Add the flour, salt, and baking soda and sift together. Dump the flour mixture into the mixing bowl and beat into the butter mixture. Remove the bowl from the machine and with a wooden spoon stir in the chocolate and nuts. Grease two large cookie sheets with the remaining 2 tablespoons of butter. Drop the cookie batter onto the sheets with a tablespoon, leaving 1½ inches or so for spreading. Bake on the middle shelf of the oven for 10 to 12 minutes. Remove the cookies to a wire rack to cool.

*A*PPLE *B*EIGNETS

This is a good dessert for brunch or lunch. It also goes nicely with roast loin of pork. Simply eliminate the apricot sauce and confectioner's sugar.

SERVES 4 TO 6

1 cup all-purpose flour
½ cup cornstarch
1½ cups beer
4 Golden Delicious apples, not quite ripe
½ cup sugar mixed with ½ teaspoon cinnamon
1 cup apricot preserves
2 tablespoons cognac or dark rum
Vegetable oil for deep-fat frying
Confectioner's sugar

Sift the flour with the cornstarch into a large bowl. Gradually stir in the beer and set aside.

Peel and core the apples and cut ½ inch off each end. Slice the apples into ⅓-inch-thick rings. Place the sugar-cinnamon mixture on a plate. Dredge the apple slices in the mixture and set aside.

Heat the apricot preserves in a small, heavy saucepan until melted. Strain the preserves through a wire strainer into a small bowl, pushing with the back of a wooden spoon. Stir in the cognac or the dark rum and set aside.

PREHEAT THE OVEN TO LOW

Fill a large cast-iron skillet one-third full of the vegetable oil. Using a deep-fat-frying thermometer, heat the oil to 375°F.

One at a time, dip the apple rings into the beer batter, allowing the excess batter to fall back into the bowl, then gently lower the apple rings into the hot oil. Fry the beignets 3 or 4 at a time for about 3 to 4 minutes

310

on each side, or until they are a light golden brown. Keep the beignets warm on a jelly roll pan lined with paper towels in the warm oven. Continue in this manner until all the apple slices are fried.

Serve the beignets on a large platter lined with paper doilies. Sprinkle with confectioner's sugar and serve the apricot sauce on the side.

CARNIVAL JELLY DOUGHNUTS

Jelly doughnuts, like the French Crullers on page 324, really must be made at home to be of excellent quality.

MAKES ABOUT 24 DOUGHNUTS

1 envelope active dry yeast
A pinch of salt
3 tablespoons sugar
¼ cup warm water (110° to 115°F)
3 to 4 cups all-purpose flour
¼ teaspoon salt
8 egg yolks, lightly beaten
½ cup milk
1 tablespoon lemon juice
1 teaspoon freshly grated orange rind
1 teaspoon vanilla extract
1½ cups raspberry preserves
2½ cups lard
Confectioner's sugar

Stir the yeast, pinch of salt, and sugar into the warm water. Let the mixture stand until it foams, about 4 to 6 minutes.

Place 3 cups of the flour into a large mixing bowl, add the salt, the yeast mixture, egg yolks, milk, lemon juice, grated orange rind, and vanilla extract. With a wooden spoon, stir all the ingredients together until the liquid is absorbed by the flour. Remove the dough from the bowl and place it on a lightly floured work surface.

Knead the dough by pushing it forward and folding it back on top of itself. Continue to knead the dough for 15 to 20 minutes, or until it is smooth and elastic. If necessary, sprinkle the dough with enough additional flour to keep it from sticking to your hands or the work surface.

Place the dough in a large buttered bowl and turn to coat it all over. Cover the bowl with plastic wrap and let it rise at room temperature for about 1 hour, or until it doubles in size. Punch the dough down in the bowl, coat it well with butter again, and let it rise for a second time until double in size, about 45 minutes.

On a lightly floured surface, roll the dough out until it is ½ inch thick. Let the dough rest for 2 minutes. Using a 2½-inch cookie cutter, cut the dough into as many disks as possible. With your fingers make 1-inch round indentations in the center of each disk and fill it with about ½ teaspoon of the raspberry preserves. Lift the dough up and pinch the edges to encase the filling. Place the doughnuts seam side down, about 2 inches apart, on a cookie sheet lined with parchment or wax paper. Let them rise for about 30 minutes, or until they double in size.

Melt the lard in a large cast-iron skillet. It should not be less than 2½ inches in depth; add more lard if necessary. Heat the lard to 325°F using a deep-fat-frying thermometer. Lower 3 or 4 of the doughnuts into the hot lard. Fry for 3 to 4 minutes, then turn them with tongs and continue to fry until they are golden brown. Transfer them to paper towels to drain.

When the doughnuts have cooled to room temperature, dust them lightly with confectioner's sugar.

Basic Sponge Roll

This cake is interchangeable with the Sponge Cake on page 315, depending on what shape cake you wish to serve.

MAKES 8 SERVINGS

4 eggs at room temperature, separated
½ teaspoon vanilla
⅓ cup sugar
⅓ cup flour, sifted

PREHEAT THE OVEN TO 350°F

Butter a 11 x 16-inch jelly roll pan and line it with wax paper.

Beat the egg yolks until light and fluffy, then add the vanilla. Beat the egg whites into soft peaks; fold into yolk mixture. Fold in the sifted flour and spread the batter on the prepared jelly roll pan. Bake for 18 to 20 minutes in the preheated oven, or until the cake shrinks slightly away from the sides of the pan. Cool on a rack.

Basic Sponge Roll may be filled with fresh fruit and whipped cream or with butter cream. For filling and rolling instructions see Chocolate Roulade, page 318.

$\mathscr{S}$PONGE $\mathscr{C}$AKE

Many desserts can be made from this basic cake. Slice the layers horizontally and spread on the Pastry Cream on page 334, or use it as a base for strawberry or peach shortcake.

MAKES TWO 9-INCH LAYERS

1 tablespoon softened butter
2 tablespoons plus 1¼ cups flour
5 eggs, separated
1 cup sugar
½ teaspoon salt
1 teaspoon vanilla
3 tablespoons water
Confectioner's sugar

PREHEAT THE OVEN TO 350°F

Coat the bottom and sides of two 9-inch cake pans with the softened butter. Sprinkle 1 tablespoon of the flour in each pan to coat the bottom and sides. Invert the pans and tap them to remove the excess flour. In an electric mixer, beat the egg yolks, ¾ cup of sugar, the salt, vanilla, and water until the mixture is light and thick. Fold in the 1¼ cups of flour with a large rubber spatula. Beat the egg whites until frothy, gradually add the remaining sugar, and continue to beat the egg whites until stiff. With a large rubber spatula, gently but thoroughly fold the egg whites into the yolk mixture. Scrape the batter into the prepared pans, smooth the top with the spatula, and bake on the middle shelf of the oven for 25 to 30 minutes, or until the cake tester comes out clean.

Remove from the oven and turn the cakes out onto a rack to cool. Just before serving, sprinkle with confectioner's sugar.

ℬLUEBERRY 𝒮HORTCAKE

This is a nice change from the usual strawberry shortcake. Also, if you wish, you can top the cake with a little cinnamon sugar.

MAKES 4 TO 6 SERVINGS

CAKE

- 3 cups all-purpose flour
- 3½ teaspoons double-acting baking powder
- 1½ teaspoons salt
- 4 tablespoons granulated sugar
- 8 tablespoons unsalted butter, cut into small pieces
- 1¼ cups heavy cream
- 1 tablespoon softened butter

FILLING

- ⅔ cup sugar mixed with ¼ teaspoon cinnamon
- ¾ cup water
- 1½ pints fresh blueberries, washed and picked over
- ½ teaspoon grated lemon rind

TO MAKE THE CAKE

PREHEAT THE OVEN TO 400°F

Lightly butter and flour a large cookie sheet. Sift the flour, baking powder, salt, and sugar into a large bowl. Add the butter and with your fingers rub the ingredients together until they turn into coarse, separate pieces. Stir in the heavy cream with a wooden spoon and mix until a soft dough is formed. Turn the dough out onto a lightly floured board and knead it just 1 minute. Divide the dough, making one portion a little larger than the other. Roll the larger portion into a round ½ inch thick **and place**

316

it on the cookie sheet. Spread the 1 tablespoon of softened butter on top. Roll the second piece of dough into a round a little less than ½ inch thick and place it on top of the first piece. Bake on the middle shelf of the pre-heated oven for 20 minutes, or until firm.

TO MAKE THE FILLING

Place the sugar-cinnamon mixture in a small saucepan, add the water, and cook over low heat until the sugar has dissolved. Add the blueberries and lemon rind and cook for 2 to 3 minutes, or until the berries become slightly soft. Remove from the heat and transfer the blueberry filling to a small bowl; allow it to cool to room temperature. Remove the top layer of the cake and spread the blueberry filling on the bottom layer. Replace the top layer and serve the shortcake with whipped cream or vanilla ice cream.

CHOCOLATE ROULADE

This is by far the most popular dessert in my restaurant. We serve more than six thousand portions every year. Because there is no flour in the recipe, the cake must be eaten the day it is made.

SERVES 8

CAKE

8 ounces semisweet chocolate, coarsely chopped
3 tablespoons strong black coffee
6 eggs, separated
¾ cup sugar
1 teaspoon vanilla extract
2 tablespoons unsweetened cocoa

FILLING

1½ cups chilled heavy cream (whipping cream)
3 tablespoons confectioner's sugar, sifted
2 tablespoons brandy
½ teaspoon vanilla extract

CHOCOLATE GLAZE

6 ounces semisweet chocolate
2 tablespoons strong black coffee
2 tablespoons softened butter
1 tablespoon honey
½ cup toasted, sliced almonds

TO MAKE THE CAKE
PREHEAT THE OVEN TO 350°F

Line an 11 x 17-inch jelly roll pan with wax paper, then grease the paper with butter. Set aside. Combine the chocolate and the coffee in a small, heavy saucepan. Place over the lowest possible heat until the chocolate has melted. Stir with a wooden spoon until the mixture is smooth. Remove from the heat and allow the chocolate to come to room temperature.

Beat the egg yolks with an electric mixer and gradually add ½ cup of the sugar. Continue to beat the mixture until it resembles mayonnaise. Add the vanilla, then beat in the cooled chocolate. Beat the egg whites until they are frothy, then gradually add the remaining ¼ cup of sugar and continue to beat the whites until they hold stiff peaks. Stir a large kitchen spoonful of egg whites into the chocolate mixture, then pour the chocolate over the remaining egg whites. Using a large rubber spatula fold them together quickly and thoroughly. Scrape the batter into the prepared jelly roll pan and bake on the middle shelf of the preheated oven for 15 to 17 minutes, or until the cake shrinks slightly from the sides of the pan.

Remove the pan from the oven and place on a cake rack to cool before removing the cake from the pan.

Place a large piece of parchment paper on your work surface and sift the cocoa on top. Invert the cake onto the parchment paper and remove the wax paper lining.

TO MAKE THE FILLING

Beat the cream in an electric mixer on low speed until soft peaks form. Gradually add the confectioner's sugar, then the brandy, and vanilla and continue to beat until the cream is stiff.

With a metal icing spatula spread the cream filling evenly over the cake. Using the parchment paper as an aid, roll the cake jelly roll fashion from the long side and place it on a serving platter.

TO MAKE THE CHOCOLATE GLAZE

Combine the chocolate, coffee, butter, and honey in a small, heavy saucepan. Place over the lowest possible heat until the chocolate has melted. Stir with a wooden spoon until the mixture is smooth. When the mixture has cooled to room temperature and is still fluid, pour it over the roulade, sprinkle with the toasted almond slices, and refrigerate.

Remove from the refrigerator ½ hour before serving.

$\mathcal{W}$ALNUT $\mathcal{R}$OLL

*For an interesting variation, make the Walnut Roll and the Choco-
late Roulade on page 318. With the Walnut Roll as the base, spread either
the walnut filling or the roulade filling over it, place the chocolate cake on
top, and cut into squares.*

SERVES 8

WALNUT ROLL

5 eggs, separated
¾ cup sugar
1 cup ground walnuts

WALNUT FILLING

½ cup milk
1½ cups ground walnuts
¼ pound unsalted butter
⅔ cup sugar
2 tablespoons Vanilla Brandy (page 335)
1 cup heavy cream, whipped
Confectioner's sugar

TO MAKE THE WALNUT ROLL
PREHEAT THE OVEN TO 375°F

Butter a jelly roll pan and line it with wax paper. Beat the egg yolks,
gradually adding ½ cup of the sugar. Add the walnuts and mix well. Beat
the egg whites with the remaining ¼ cup of sugar until very stiff. Fold the
whites into the nut mixture and spread evenly in the prepared pan. Bake
for about 15 minutes, or until the cake shrinks slightly away from the sides
of the pan. Cool on a rack.

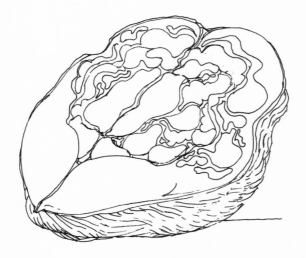

TO MAKE THE WALNUT FILLING

Bring the milk to a boil, pour it over the walnuts, and cool to room temperature. Cream the butter with the sugar. Beat in the cooled nut mixture and the cognac. Fold in the whipped cream. Spread the filling evenly on the cooled cake and roll up jelly roll fashion. Before serving, sprinkle with confectioner's sugar.

*L*A *S*ALLE *C*HEESECAKE

This cheesecake recipe is from the once-famous La Salle Hotel in Chicago. It was given to my friend Margaret Platt by a cousin of hers who was, for many years, an entertainer at the hotel, and Margaret, in turn, gave it to me.

I have made many cheesecakes and read many different recipes, but have never come across a recipe that called for a syrup to be beaten into the egg whites. It is actually an Italian meringue. It controls the rising of the egg whites and eliminates cracking. This recipe does not call for lemon; however, if you wish, you may add to the cake batter 2 teaspoons of freshly grated lemon rind.

SERVES 10 TO 12

2 *pounds baker's or farmer's cheese, at room temperature*
1/2 *cup plus 2 tablespoons cornstarch*
8 *eggs, separated*
A pinch of salt
1 *tablespoon pure vanilla extract*
1 *cup water*
1 1/3 *cups granulated sugar*
1 *tablespoon butter, softened*

PREHEAT THE OVEN TO 350°F

Fit an electric mixer with a paddle (or do this by hand with a whisk). Place the cheese in the mixing bowl and beat on medium speed. Sift in the cornstarch and mix well. Add the egg yolks, one at a time, beating well after each addition, then add the salt and vanilla and continue to beat until the mixture is light and smooth.

Place the egg whites in a clean bowl and fit the machine with the whip.

Combine the water and sugar in a small saucepan and cook over low heat until the sugar dissolves. Bring the water to a boil and boil for 5 minutes.

Gradually beat the egg whites to soft peaks and in a thin stream add the syrup as you continue to beat the whites. When the syrup has been incorporated, continue to beat the mixture until it cools to room temperature. Fold the meringue into the yolk mixture thoroughly (no egg whites should be visible).

Grease a 10-inch spring form pan with the softened butter. Scrape the cake mixture into the spring form pan and place it in a shallow roasting pan filled with 1 inch of water. Bake the cheesecake on the middle shelf of the oven for 55 minutes. Remove from the oven and cool the cake in the pan on a wire rack. Chill the cheesecake in the refrigerator for several hours before serving.

*F*RENCH *C*RULLERS

This is a childhood favorite of mine. The best are the ones you make yourself. Cruller dough and cream puff pastry are exactly the same.

MAKES ABOUT 18 CRULLERS

1 cup milk
⅛ teaspoon salt
1 tablespoon sugar
1 teaspoon grated lemon rind
6 tablespoons unsalted butter
1 cup all-purpose flour, sifted
4 eggs, beaten
Vegetable oil for deep-fat frying
Confectioner's sugar

Combine the milk, salt, sugar, lemon rind, and butter in a 1-quart saucepan. Bring the mixture to a boil over high heat and when the butter has melted, remove the saucepan from the heat. Dump in the sifted flour all at once, return the pan to low heat, and with a wooden spoon beat the mixture until it no longer clings to the bottom or sides of the saucepan.

Remove the saucepan from the heat and make a well in the center of the dough. Gradually beat the beaten eggs into the center of the well with a wooden spoon until they have been completely incorporated. Pack the dough into a large pastry bag fitted with a large star tip.

Fill a large cast-iron skillet two-thirds full of vegetable oil. Using a deep-fat-frying thermometer heat the oil to 365°F. Press 3-inch circles onto a slotted spatula and gently lower the dough into the hot fat. Fry about 3 crullers at a time, turning them once or twice, until they are golden brown. Drain the crullers on a cake rack over a jelly roll pan lined with paper towels.

When the crullers have cooled to room temperature, dust them with confectioner's sugar.

$\mathscr{S}$NIPDOODLE

This true American cake entered my life in 1955. The recipe came from the late Robert Stevenson, creator of Chillingsworth, the restaurant on Cape Cod where I enjoyed working as chef for five summers. There is nothing that goes better with a hot cup of tea than Snipdoodle.

MAKES ONE 8-INCH CAKE

½ cup vegetable shortening
1¼ cups sugar
2 eggs
1½ cups all-purpose flour
2 teaspoons baking powder
¼ teaspoon salt
1¼ cups milk
2 tablespoons sugar plus ½ teaspoon cinnamon, mixed

PREHEAT THE OVEN TO 350°F

Lightly butter and flour an 8 x 8 x 2-inch baking pan.

With an electric mixer cream the vegetable shortening and sugar together until light and fluffy. Beat in the eggs one at a time until they are thoroughly incorporated.

Sift the flour, baking powder, and salt onto a strip of wax paper. Beat one-third of this mixture into the egg mixture. Then beat in one-third of the milk. Continue alternating the flour and the milk, one-third at a time, beating until the batter is smooth.

Pour the batter into the prepared baking pan and bake on the middle shelf of the preheated oven for about 30 minutes, or until a cake tester comes out clean. Remove the cake from the oven and while it is still warm sprinkle the surface with the cinnamon-sugar mixture. When the cake is cool enough to handle, cut into 2-inch squares, using a metal icing spatula to remove them from the pan.

Sacher Torte

This torte is probably the most famous of them all. Twenty years ago it would have been very difficult to find a Sacher Torte in a bakery. Now it is quite common. I read in one book that the recipe is a closely guarded secret of the Sacher Hotel in Vienna. Another author wrote, "I met a pastry chef from the Sacher Hotel and he gave me the recipe." Here's my version, and I hope you enjoy it!

MAKES 1 SACHER TORTE OR 8 TO 10 SERVINGS

CAKE

- 6 *tablespoons unsalted butter*
- ¾ *cup granulated sugar*
- 8 *eggs, separated*
- 1¼ *cups all-purpose flour, sifted*
- 8 *ounces semisweet chocolate, melted and cooled*
- 1⅓ *cups apricot preserves, rubbed through a sieve with the back of a wooden spoon*

CHOCOLATE GLAZE

- 8 *ounces semisweet chocolate, chopped*
- 4 *tablespoons softened butter*
- 3 *tablespoons honey*
- ½ *teaspoon vanilla*

TO MAKE THE CAKE
PREHEAT THE OVEN TO 350°F

Grease and flour a 9-inch spring form pan. In an electric mixer, cream the butter with ½ cup of the sugar until the mixture is light and fluffy. Gradually add the egg yolks, one at a time, beating well after each

326

addition. Add the flour and mix in the cooled melted chocolate. Beat the egg whites until frothy. Gradually add the remaining ¼ cup of sugar and continue to beat the whites until stiff.

Mix one-quarter of the beaten egg whites into the chocolate mixture, then pour into the remaining egg whites. With a large rubber spatula, fold the whites and chocolate mixture together gently but thoroughly. Pour the cake batter into the prepared spring form pan.

Bake on the middle shelf of the preheated oven for 30 to 40 minutes, or until a cake tester inserted in the middle of the cake comes out clean. Cook the cake for 10 minutes on a wire rack. Remove the pan and let the cake cool to room temperature.

Cut the cake in half horizontally. Spread the bottom layer with ⅓ cup of the apricot preserves. Replace the top layer and coat the sides and top of the cake with the remaining preserves. Refrigerate the torte until the apricot glaze is firm.

TO MAKE THE CHOCOLATE GLAZE

Place the chocolate, butter, honey, and vanilla in a small, heavy saucepan and set over the lowest heat possible. Mix the glaze with a wooden spoon until the chocolate has melted and all the ingredients are well blended. Set a wire rack on a jelly roll pan. Place the cooled cake on the rack. Pour the glaze evenly over the cake. Return the cake to the refrigerator. Scrape up the excess chocolate from the jelly roll pan and fill a paper cone with it. Cut off a very small tip from the cone and when the glaze on the cake has hardened write SACHER on the top!

ℋUCKLEBERRY ℘IE

I recall picking these berries as a child for my mother in the woods. She would turn them into wonderful muffins and pies. If you live in a area where huckleberries are not available fresh or frozen, you can use blueberries.

Recently I was served Huckleberry Pie made with frozen berries; I could not tell the difference.

MAKES ONE 9-INCH PIE

PIE

6 cups huckleberries, fresh or frozen and thawed
1½ cups sugar mixed with 2 tablespoons tapioca
1½ teaspoons fresh lemon juice
1½ recipes Flaky Pastry Crust (page 332)

GLAZE

1 egg
2 tablespoons heavy cream
2 teaspoons sugar mixed with ¼ teaspoon cinnamon

TO MAKE THE PIE

Put the berries in a colander and wash them under cold running water. Remove all stems and any unripe or bruised berries. Shake the colander to remove any excess water. Mix the sugar-tapioca and the lemon juice with the berries and set aside.

Butter a 9-inch pie plate and set aside.

Remove the pastry from the refrigerator and divide it in half. Shape each half into a thick, round cake. On a lightly floured surface roll one piece of pastry into an 11-inch round. Brush off any excess flour from the pastry.

328

Roll the pastry onto the rolling pin and unroll it over the pie plate. Gently fit the pastry into the pie plate.

Put the berry mixture on top of the pastry. Roll out the second piece of pastry, and in the same manner roll the pastry on top of the berries. Press the two layers of pastry together, and with a sharp paring knife strip off any excess pastry from the edge of the plate. With the tines of a fork press the edges of the pastry against the pie plate. Place the prepared pie in the refrigerator to rest for 30 minutes.

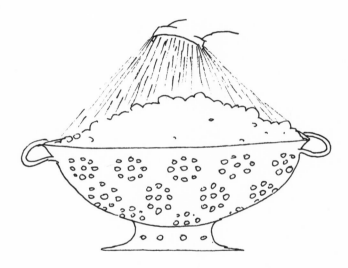

TO MAKE THE GLAZE AND BAKE THE PIE

PREHEAT THE OVEN TO 400°F

Remove the pie from the refrigerator. Beat the egg and cream together and brush it on top of the pie. Sprinkle with the cinnamon-sugar and cut a 1-inch hole in the center to form a vent for the steam to escape.

Place the pie on the middle shelf of the oven. Reduce the heat to 375° and bake for 35 to 45 minutes, or until the crust is a deep golden brown.

Remove to a wire rack and let the pie cool to room temperature.

DEEP DISH APPLE PIE

Cooking the apples in the unsalted butter for a few minutes is what makes this pie unique. If you have made the Vanilla Brandy on page 335 by all means use it.

SERVES 6

1/4 cup unsalted butter
3 pounds Granny Smith apples, peeled, cored, and cut into 1/2-inch-thick
      slices
1/2 cup plus 1 tablespoon sugar
2 teaspoons vanilla extract
1 recipe Cream Cheese Pastry (page 331)
Milk

PREHEAT THE OVEN TO 400°F

Melt the butter in a large skillet. Add the sliced apples and cook them for 5 minutes. Stir in the 1/2 cup of sugar, remove from the heat, and stir in the vanilla. Set aside to cool. Then scrape the mixture into a 9-inch pie plate.

On a lightly floured surface, roll the pastry into an 11-inch round. Brush off any excess flour from the pastry. Roll the pastry onto the rolling pin and unroll it over the pie plate. With a paring knife, trim off any excess pastry from the edge of the pie plate. With the tines of a fork, press the edges of the pastry against the pie plate. Cut a 1-inch hole in the middle of the pastry, creating a vent for the steam to escape. Brush the surface with a little milk and sprinkle with the remaining 1 tablespoon of sugar. Place the pie on the middle shelf of the preheated oven. Reduce the heat to 375° and bake the pie for 30 to 40 minutes, or until the crust is a deep golden brown. Remove to a wire rack to cool to room temperature before serving.

CREAM CHEESE PASTRY

This pastry is not only easy to make but also easy to roll out. Since there isn't any liquid in the pastry, the gluten never becomes activated. If you wish to use it for a savory pie, simply eliminate the sugar.

MAKES ONE 9-INCH SHELL OR 1 TOP FOR A DEEP DISH PIE

1½ *cups all-purpose flour*
¼ *teaspoon salt*
1 *tablespoon sugar*
6 *tablespoons unsalted butter*
One 3-ounce package of cream cheese, at room temperature

Combine the flour, salt, and sugar in the container of an electric mixer fitted with a paddle (or do this by hand with a whisk). Mix the dry ingredients together at low speed. Add the butter and cream cheese and mix on medium speed until the ingredients are well blended. Wrap the pastry in wax paper and chill for 30 minutes before rolling it out.

Flaky Pastry Crust

This is the recipe I taught for many years in my baking classes. If using this pastry for a quiche, omit the sugar. For a two-crust pie, make one and a half times the recipe.

MAKES ONE 9-INCH PIE SHELL

1½ cups all-purpose flour
¼ teaspoon salt
2 teaspoons sugar
6 tablespoons unsalted butter, chilled and cut into small pieces
2 tablespoons chilled vegetable shortening
Ice water

Place the flour in a medium-sized bowl, add the salt, sugar, butter, and shortening. Rub the ingredients together between your fingertips, working quickly—the mixture will soon turn into granules. Sprinkle with 3 tablespoons of ice water. Work the water into the granules and gather the mass into a ball. If the dough crumbles, add another tablespoon of ice water. The amount of water needed for 1½ cups of flour can range from 3 to 5 tablespoons, depending upon the moisture content of the flour. Press the ball of pastry into a thick cake and wrap it in plastic. Let the pastry chill and rest in the refrigerator for at least 30 minutes before rolling.

Remove the pastry from the refrigerator. On a lightly floured surface, roll the pastry into an 11-inch round. Brush off any excess flour from the pastry. Roll the pastry onto the rolling pin and unroll it over the pie plate. With a paring knife, trim off any excess pastry from the edge of the pie plate.

Place the pastry-lined pie plate in the refrigerator to chill and rest for 20 minutes.

PREHEAT THE OVEN TO 400°F

Remove the unbaked pastry shell from the refrigerator and fit a piece of heavy-duty aluminum foil on top. Bake on the middle shelf of the preheated oven for 12 minutes. Remove the foil and prick the pastry in two or three places with the tines of a fork. Continue to bake the shell for 8 minutes, or until the crust is golden brown.

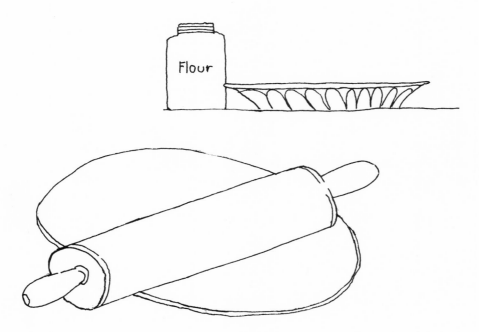

$\mathscr{P}$ASTRY $\mathscr{C}$REAM

Unlike pastry creams with gelatin, which must be used immediately, this one can be made the day before. Don't worry about bringing the mixture to a boil. The cornstarch will keep the egg yolks from curdling.

MAKES ONE 9-INCH TART SHELL

¼ cup granulated sugar
2 tablespoons cornstarch
A pinch of salt
2 egg yolks
1 cup milk
½ teaspoon vanilla extract

Combine the sugar, cornstarch, and salt in a small, heavy saucepan (not aluminum) and shake the saucepan to make sure the ingredients are mixed well. Add the egg yolks and stir with a wooden spoon until the mixture turns into a smooth paste. Whisk in the milk and bring to a boil. Remove from the heat, add the vanilla, and pour into a small bowl. Cover the Pastry Cream with plastic wrap and place in the refrigerator to chill.

$\mathscr{V}$ANILLA $\mathscr{B}$RANDY

Use Vanilla Brandy in place of vanilla extract. If you make desserts and bake frequently you will find it can be less expensive.

MAKES ONE FIFTH

2 bottles brandy
8 vanilla beans

Stick the vanilla beans into a bottle of brandy. Let sit for 2 weeks.

As the Vanilla Brandy is used, 1 or 2 tablespoons at a time, replenish it from the second bottle.

CHOCOLATE MOUSSE

This is one of a few chocolate mousse recipes that can be unmolded. You can pipe whipped cream on top and decorate it with candied violets, or serve it with the Almond Custard Sauce on page 296.

SERVES 6 TO 8

8 ounces semisweet chocolate, chopped into small pieces
2 tablespoons strong black coffee
4 egg yolks
⅓ cup sugar
3 tablespoons Grand Marnier
8 tablespoons softened butter
2 tablespoons finely chopped glazed orange peel
5 egg whites

Very lightly oil a 1-quart charlotte mold with vegetable oil or preferably with sweet almond oil.

Melt the chocolate with the coffee over very low heat. Combine the egg yolks, sugar, and Grand Marnier in the bowl of an electric mixer set in a pan of simmering water. Beat the mixture with a wire whisk until it is very hot. Remove the bowl from the hot water and beat on high speed until the mixture is very thick and has cooled to room temperature.

Beat in the chocolate mixture, the softened butter, and the glazed orange peel. Beat the egg whites until stiff. Mix one-quarter of the egg whites into the chocolate mixture, then, with a rubber spatula, fold in the remaining egg whites gently but thoroughly.

Scrape the mousse into the prepared mold. Tap the mold gently on the counter. Cover with plastic wrap and chill in the refrigerator for at least 3 hours.

Remove the plastic wrap and invert a serving dish on top of the mold. Turn the plate and mold over. If the mousse doesn't unmold, wipe it with a hot, wet towel.

Serve with fresh whipped cream.

CRÈME BRÛLÉE

This creamy, rich dessert was very popular back in the 1950's. Then the world became cholesterol conscious. For some reason it is once again gaining in popularity. Although this recipe has a French name, its origins are in England, where granulated sugar is used for caramelizing. I prefer brown sugar.

SERVES 6

6 egg yolks
4 tablespoons granulated sugar
A pinch of salt
3 cups heavy cream, heated
1 teaspoon vanilla extract
½ cup light brown sugar

PREHEAT THE OVEN TO 350°F

With an electric mixer beat the egg yolks with the granulated sugar and the salt until the mixture resembles mayonnaise. Gradually add the heated cream. Add the vanilla and strain the mixture through a fine sieve into a 1-quart soufflé dish. Place the soufflé dish in a small roasting pan and fill the pan two-thirds full of hot water. Bake on the middle shelf of the preheated oven for 45 minutes to 1 hour, or until a knife inserted in the center comes out clean. Remove the dish from the water and cool to room temperature. Cover the soufflé dish and chill 4 to 6 hours, or until it is very cold.

PREHEAT THE BROILER

Force the light brown sugar through a fine sieve with the back of a wooden spoon, covering the surface of the crème evenly. Place the soufflé dish under the broiler 4 inches from the heat to caramelize the sugar topping. This should not take more than 5 minutes.

𝒯URIN 𝓛OAF

This is a dense, rich dessert. You will reduce the richness by serving it with whipped cream, or the Almond Custard Sauce on page 296, to cut the sweetness of the chocolate.

SERVES 6 TO 8

4 ounces bittersweet chocolate, chopped
2 tablespoons strong black coffee
½ cup sifted confectioner's sugar
8 tablespoons unsalted butter
2 teaspoons Vanilla Brandy (page 335)
One 1-pound can unsweetened chestnut purée

Melt the chocolate with the coffee in a small, heavy saucepan. Remove from the heat and beat in the sifted confectioner's sugar, butter, and brandy. Combine this mixture with the chestnut purée.

Lightly oil a 9 x 5 x 3-inch loaf pan with vegetable oil, then line the pan with wax paper. Fill the pan with the chestnut mixture and place it in the refrigerator for 3 to 4 hours, or until the mixture is firm. Invert the Turin Loaf on a platter and slice it as you would a pound cake.

ℤABAGLIONE

Zabaglione is served warm or cold, and often with strawberries. It is also wonderful with fresh sliced peaches.

SERVES 4 TO 6

6 egg yolks
⅓ cup granulated sugar
½ cup sweet Marsala wine

Combine the egg yolks, sugar, and Marsala wine in a stainless steel mixing bowl. Place the bowl over a pan of barely simmering water. With a wire balloon whisk, beat the mixture until it triples in volume.

339

*A*MARETTO *S*ORBET

This recipe was created in my kitchen workshop for Amaretto di Saronno. Because water qualities vary throughout the United States, non-effervescent mineral water was used to assure the proper consistency.

SERVES 6 TO 8

SORBET

1 cup noneffervescent mineral water
1⅓ cups sugar syrup (see below)
½ cup plus 2 tablespoons Amaretto liqueur
6 tablespoons fresh lemon juice
1 egg white

SUGAR SYRUP
(MAKES ABOUT 1 QUART)

1¼ cups granulated sugar
1 cup noneffervescent mineral water

TO MAKE THE SORBET

Combine the mineral water, syrup, Amaretto, and lemon juice in a medium-sized bowl. Cover with plastic wrap and chill in the refrigerator until the mixture is very cold. Pour the chilled Amaretto mixture into an ice cream freezer and freeze the sorbet according to the directions on the machine. When the sorbet begins to set, remove 2 tablespoons and beat it with the egg white; return to the machine. When the sorbet is set, remove it from the ice cream maker, place it in a large, cold bowl, and beat with a large, stiff whisk.

Scrape the sorbet into a storage container with a tight-fitting cover and place it in the freezer until ready to serve.

TO MAKE THE SUGAR SYRUP

Combine the granulated sugar and the water in a small saucepan. Place the mixture over low heat and stir with a wooden spoon until the sugar dissolves. Raise the heat to high and bring the syrup to a boil. Immediately remove from the heat and set the syrup aside to cool to room temperature.

$\mathscr{B}$ISCUIT $\mathscr{T}$ORTONI

In restaurants this dessert is served in little paper cups and is always made with rum flavoring. Using real dark rum and shaping the mixture in a spring form pan makes a world of difference.

SERVES 8 TO 12

1 quart chilled heavy cream
¾ cup confectioner's sugar plus 2 tablespoons
⅛ teaspoon salt
16 Amaretto macaroons, crushed in a food processor
⅔ cup dark rum
2 teaspoons vanilla extract
½ cup toasted sliced almonds

Line the bottom and sides of a 9- or 10-inch spring form pan with wax paper. Use a little vegetable oil to make the paper cling to the sides of the pan. Place in the freezer until ready to use.

Beat the heavy cream in a chilled bowl with an electric mixer, gradually adding the ¾ cup of confectioner's sugar and the salt, until it thickens into soft mounds.

With a large rubber spatula fold in the crushed Amaretto macaroons, the rum, and the vanilla extract. Scrape the cream mixture into the prepared spring form pan. Sprinkle with the toasted almonds and freeze the Biscuit Tortoni for 4 to 6 hours, or until firm. Just before serving, release it from the pan and with a large metal spatula remove it from the bottom of the form and place it on a chilled serving plate. Sift the remaining 2 tablespoons of confectioner's sugar over the top and serve.

ORANGE ICE

If you don't have extra ice cube trays, I suggest pouring the mixture into freezer zip-lock bags, which work very well.

SERVES 4 TO 6

3 cups water
2 cups sugar
2 tablespoons clear Karo syrup
2 cups fresh orange juice
2 tablespoons fresh lemon juice

Combine the water, sugar, and Karo syrup in a 2-quart saucepan. Cook over low heat until the sugar dissolves. Raise the heat and bring the mixture to a rolling boil. Boil for 5 minutes, remove from the heat, and cool the syrup to room temperature. Stir in the orange and lemon juices. Pour the mixture into several ice cube trays and place in the freezer. When the liquid turns to ice, release the cubes and store in plastic bags.

To serve, crush the ice in a food processor and mound in champagne glasses. If you wish, you can reinforce it with a dribble or two of Grand Marnier.

$\mathscr{B}$AKED $\mathscr{A}$PPLES

Because I feel Cortland apples make a most attractive dessert, they are my preference. You can also use Rome Beautys or Jonathans.

SERVES 6

APPLES

2 cups water
1 cup sugar
1 cinnamon stick
2 cloves
6 large apples, Rome Beauty, Jonathan, or Cortland, cored

FILLING

1½ cups toasted almonds
2 teaspoons grated lemon rind
¼ cup sugar
4 tablespoons butter
2 egg yolks
½ teaspoon vanilla extract

TO PREPARE THE APPLES
PREHEAT THE OVEN TO 375°F

Combine the water, sugar, cinnamon stick, and cloves in a small saucepan. Cook the mixture over low heat until the sugar dissolves. Raise the heat and bring the mixture to a boil. Boil for 10 minutes and remove from the heat.

Place the apples in a shallow baking dish, stem side down. Strain the syrup over the apples and discard the cinnamon stick and cloves. Bake the apples on the middle shelf of the oven for 20 minutes. Remove the apples from the oven and turn them over.

TO MAKE THE FILLING AND ASSEMBLE

Combine the toasted almonds, lemon rind, sugar, butter, and egg yolks in the container of a food processor. Process the mixture until it turns into a paste. Transfer the mixture to a pastry bag fitted with a ½-inch plain tube. Force some of the almond mixture into each apple core. Return the apples to the oven and bake them for an additional 20 minutes, until they are soft.

Transfer the apples to a serving dish and stir the vanilla extract into the syrup remaining in the baking dish. Pour the syrup over the apples and chill them in the refrigerator before serving.

$\mathscr{S}$TRAWBERRIES $\mathscr{E}$AST *37* TH $\mathscr{S}$TREET

You can simply call this strawberries with honey and pistachios, but the reason for my name is as follows. Many years ago, during the winter months off from my job on Cape Cod, I periodically did catering work. A client on East 37th Street in New York City had this recipe handed down from her grandmother; obviously I still remember it.

SERVES 4 TO 6

1 quart ripe strawberries
¼ cup currant jelly
½ cup honey
2 tablespoons unsalted, shelled pistachios, chopped

Wash the berries under cold running water and pat them dry with paper towels. Hull the berries, place them in a deep glass bowl, and refrigerate.

Melt the currant jelly and strain it through a wire sieve into a small bowl. Mix the honey into the currant jelly and gently stir the honey mixture into the berries. Sprinkle with the pistachios and serve.

$\mathscr{I}$NDEX

347

Cole slaw, 271
Cookies, chocolate chip, 309
Corn
chowder, 71
and green chile soufflé, 205
Cornbread, skillet, 308
Crabmeat rémoulade, 16–17
Cream cheese pastry, 331
Crème brûlée, 337
Croissants, 302–303
Croustades, 28–31
crab or lobster, 31
mushroom, 28–30
Crullers, French, 324
Cucumber(s)
au gratin, 207–208
salad, 269
soup, cold, 66
in sour cream, 270

Desserts, 309–346
apple pie, deep dish, 330
baked apples, 344–345
beignets, apple, 310–311
biscuit tortoni, 342
cakes
cheese, La Salle, 322–323
roulade, chocolate, 318–319
Sacher torte, 326–327
shortcake, blueberry, 316–317
snipdoodle, 325
sponge, 315
sponge roll, basic, 314
walnut roll, 320–321
cookies, chocolate chip, 309
crème brûlée, 337
crullers, French, 324
doughnuts, carnival jelly, 312–313
huckleberry pie, 328–329
ice, orange, 343
mousse, chocolate, 336

pastries
crust, flaky, 332–333
cream cheese, 331
pastry cream, 334
pies
apple, deep dish, 330
huckleberry, 328–329
sorbet, amaretto, 340–341
sponge roll, basic, 314
strawberries East 37th Street, 346
Turin loaf, 338
vanilla brandy, 335
zabaglione, 339
Doughnuts, carnival jelly, 312–313
Duck, broiled, marinated, 108–109
Dumplings
German potato, 219
potato, 218

Endive
creamed, with ham, 209–210
and watercress salad, 272
Escarole soup, 63
Etouffée, shrimp, 158

Filet mignon Eszterházy, 118–119
Fish. *See* Seafood
Fish stock, 45
Fisherman's stew, 177–178
Fondue, cheese, 33
Frogs legs yakitori style, 112–113
Fruit
apple pie, deep dish, 330
baked apples, 344–345
huckleberry pie, 328–329
orange ice, 343
strawberries East 37th Street, 346

Gazpacho, 70
German potato dumplings, 219
German potato salad, 275
Green pea soup, chilled, with mint, 68

Guacamole, 26
Gumbo, oyster and crab, 164–165

Haddock, smoked, quiche, 186–187
Ham, mousse of, 6
Hamburger steaks, 121
Hamburgers, 121
Herring salad, 280
Hollandaise sauce, 293
Hors d'oeuvres, 3–42
  anchovy canapés, hot, 7
  beef
    heart, skewered, 4
    spiced, 5
  bread crumbs, fresh, 12
  caponata, 24–25
  caviar, vegetable, 27
  celery Victor, 32
  ceviche, 9
  cheese
    balls, 37–38
    fondue, 33
    and green chili dip, 42
    pizza, 40–41
    soufflé, 34–35
    spread, Liptauer, 38
    squares, fried, 36–37
  chicken hearts teriyaki, 3
  clams with aspic, cherrystone, 13
  crabmeat rémoulade, 16–17
  croustades, 28–31
    crab or lobster, 31
    mushroom, 28–30
  fondue, cheese, 33
  guacamole, 26
  ham, mousse of, 6
  Liptauer cheese spread, 38
  mousse, tricolor, 14–15
  mushrooms
    Italian style, stuffed, 23
    marinated, 20
    stuffed with crab, 21–22

  oysters on the half shell, baked, 19
  shrimp
    balls, 10–11
    rémoulade, 18
    toast, 8
  vegetable caviar, 27
Huckleberry pie, 328–329

Ice, orange, 343

Kale, shredded, 211
Kohlrabi, stuffed, 212–213

Lamb, 126–131
  boiled leg with caper and parsley
    sauce, 128–129
  braised shoulder, 127
  broiled boned leg, 130
  Irish stew, 126
  roast leg, 131
Lentils with cotechino sausage, 261
Lettuce, Boston, wilted, 214
Liptauer cheese spread, 38
Lobster
  à l'Américaine, 173–174
  bisque, 54–55

Mayonnaise, 294
Meat
  beef
    filet mignon Eszterházy, 118–119
    hamburger steaks, 121
    hamburgers, 121
    heart, skewered, 4
    meat loaf with jalapeño chilies, 125
    picadillo, 120
    shell steaks in a cognac sauce, 117
    soups
      broth with marrow and chives, 59
      stock, 46–47

Vegetable(s)
  asparagus
    boiled, 199
    frittata, 200
  beef soup, German, 60–61
  broccoli Roman style, 201
  cabbage (green) in white wine, 202
  cauliflower, deep-fried, 203
  caviar, 27
  celery root and potatoes, 204
  corn and green chile soufflé, 205
  cucumbers au gratin, 207–208
  endive, creamed, with ham, 209–210
  kale, shredded, 211
  kohlrabi, stuffed, 212–213
  lettuce, Boston, wilted, 214
  mushrooms
    broiled, caps, 215
    turnips (white) and, 216
  omelet Spanish style, 237
  peas (yellow split), purée of, 226–227
  peppers, roasted, 217
  potato(es)
    dumplings, 218
    French-fried, 220–221
    German, dumplings, 219
    Parisienne, 223
    shredded, cakes, 222
    stuffed, fish house style, 224–225
  squash (summer), mashed, 229
  string beans in sour cream sauce, 228
  stuffed, Spanish style, 238–239
  succotash (summer), 230
  tomatoes
    fried, Pennsylvania Dutch, 231
    Provençale, 232
  turnips (white) and mushrooms, 216
  zucchini
    pie, 235–236
    stuffed, 233–234

Watercress, soup, cream of, 67
White bean and tuna salad, 276
White bread, 306–307

Yorkshire popovers, 299

Zabaglione, 339
Zucchini
  pie, 235–236
  stuffed, 233–234

Chef, writer, teacher, and restaurateur, JOHN CLANCY began his culinary career as a chef at Chillingsworth, a well-known restaurant on Cape Cod, and moved from there to the Coach House, in New York City. He taught for eight years with James Beard before opening his own cooking school, John Clancy's Kitchen Workshop, and traveling all over the world to teach cooking and baking. Serving as chef for the Time-Life Books Foods of the World Series, Clancy had the opportunity to become acquainted with the preparation of dishes of many ethnic varieties and national origins—an eclecticism that is reflected in *John Clancy's Favorite Recipes*. Finally, in 1981 he opened his own successful restaurant, John Clancy's, in the heart of New York's Greenwich Village. Specializing in fish and seafood, it was the first to introduce mesquite grilling on the East Coast.

JOHN CLANCY is the author of four other books, including *John Clancy's Fish Cookery* and *John Clancy's Christmas Cookbook*.

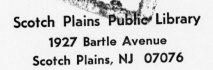